Twayne's English Authors Series

Sylvia E. Bowman, *Editor*

Indiana University

William Wycherley

 127

William Wycherley

By KATHARINE M. ROGERS

WILLIAM WYCHERLEY

TO KEN

Preface

One of the first things King Charles II did after being restored to his father's throne was to reopen the theaters, closed by Puritan edict in 1642. For a while the theaters depended on the plays of William Shakespeare, Ben Jonson, and Francis Beaumont and John Fletcher; but gradually a new type of comedy (as well as tragedy) developed that was designed to meet the tastes of a clever, aristocratic audience preoccupied with wit, breeding, and style. Like most comedy, it dealt with love—but with love that was practically stripped of romance. In such comedy, the young hero and heroine are attracted to each other, but never lose their clearness of head. The interest lies, not in lyrical romantic flights, but in brilliant contests in which each lover tries to excel the other in wit. Because Restoration comedy is not romantic, it lacks the appeal of, say, Shakespearean comedy. It does not carry us away on poetic wings nor draw us into intense sympathy for the young lovers. On the other hand, it offers us more wit and undiluted comic effect. The lovers themselves contribute to the comedy, delighting us with their wit and, sometimes, amusing us with their affectations.

Restoration comedy appeals, more than most comedy, to the intellect. The authors do not ask us to empathize with the characters but to laugh at them. Margery Pinchwife, married to an odious husband, is comic in her attempt to secure a more congenial mate; we are pleased she gets her bit of fun with Horner, but not worried about her sin of adultery nor even about what will happen to her when Pinchwife gets her back to the country. Since the author does not involve us with the characters, we perceive more clearly their ridiculous aspects; we see Margery as a demonstration of the ludicrousness of raw nature in a sophisticated setting. Restoration comedy of manners is difficult because it makes constant demands on our intellectual alertness without enlisting interest by strong appeals to our emotions. It is rewarding because it challenges our wit and because its detached tone facilitates extended, penetrating analyses of human folly.

Written for a coterie with clearly defined standards (the court circle and those who imitated them), Restoration comedy was preoccupied with fine social distinctions. The audience was keenly aware of manners and affectations, and it valued wit above all things. It considered repartee "the very soul of conversation" and therefore "the greatest grace of Comedy." The distinctive social ideal of the time was not so much the refined gentleman as the true wit. Accordingly, the conversation of witty, sophisticated ladies and gentlemen was better developed in Restoration comedy than ever before or since. So was the character of the true wit. As John Dryden said, Ben Jonson's Truewit, although "the best character of a gentleman" he ever made, is crude and labored compared to the gentlemen of Restoration comedy.[1]

Moreover, the most characteristic feature of the comedy was the contrast between the true and the would-be wit. Because the audience was so sophisticated, the playwright could make the social pretender very like the social ideal (as, in real life, he would be) and, at the same time, demonstrate the difference between true and false wit. The true wit is highly intelligent: his epigrams spring spontaneously from his thought, and his similes and paradoxes express truth rather than mere ingenuity. He has the judgment to understand himself and to know that making similes is not the main business of life. The would-be wit, on the other hand, lives to make inane similes which express insignificant resemblances instead of insight. He thinks that by concocting similes he can be a true wit himself, and he rejoices in the contemplation of his own spurious wit, breeding, and knowledge of the Town.

Members of Restoration high society provided an inspiration as well as a discriminating audience for comedy. They intensely cultivated epigrams and repartee; and Dryden, contrasting contemporary drama with that of the preceding age, hardly flattered when he wrote: "Our ladies and our men now speak more wit/In conversation, than those poets writ." [2] Concerned primarily with sophisticated courtship, polished conversation, and the realization of a social ideal, the great Restoration comedies were comedies of manners: they focused on people's behavior in their social setting, on such things as the ways in which they adjust to their society rather than on the ways in which fundamental impulses like greed can distort personality.

The comedy of manners satirizes extremes of fashion, affectations, and the conflict between nature and social façade. It studies these within the group who are aware of the conventions: "Gentlemen will now be entertained with the follies of each other," wrote Dryden.[3] Although the comedy of manners concentrates on the social surface, it is not necessarily superficial: socialization is a part of "human nature," without which man cannot exist. The comedy of manners can deal with such basic questions as the extent to which a man like Horner is distorted by his striking success in achieving the ideal of his society, or the extent to which a man like Manly should accept the insincerity inevitable in social relationships.

The comedy of manners is, however, more dependent on its particular social milieu than is the comedy of character. We can easily appreciate the manifestations of greed in Jonson's *Volpone* because greed still shows itself in essentially the same ways as in Jonson's time; it is harder to appreciate the manifestations of social affectation in George Etherege's *The Man of Mode* because, although people are still affected, they affect different qualities as social ideals change. Molière, the great contemporary of the Restoration dramatists, acknowledged this limitation when he said the business of comedy was to represent in general all the failings of men, and in particular those of one's contemporaries.[4]

The nineteenth century condemned Restoration comedy as immoral. The twentieth century, no longer upset by such things as the "ruin" of Margery Pinchwife, is more apt to condemn it as trivial and unrealistic. We do not object to the adultery and obscene speeches, but we may feel the plays have no connection with our own lives, or indeed with any important issues—that they are, in L. C. Knights' words, "trivial, gross and dull."[5]

This statement is not true, however, of the best of the plays. Most of them deal with making a suitable marriage, surely one of the most important concerns in life. They deal with it in realistic terms, representing the wariness appropriate to a man and woman making a decision that will bind them for the rest of their lives, and recognizing the existence of sexual antagonism, even between lovers. The playwrights consider courtship rationally, and adultery too. Although they often use it as a subject for titillating farce, they sometimes sensibly consider what conditions in a marriage conduce to or justify adultery. Although we no longer substitute wit and breeding for moral values, as the Restoration playwrights tended to do, their fine distinctions between true and false wit and breeding will be relevant as long as these qualities are prized in cultivated society.

The comedies would indeed be trivial if they had no connection with reality, as some critics (including an admirer, Charles Lamb) have maintained. It is true that they give an impression of artificiality. Contrived situations in which everyone is competing in wit with everyone else, in which the true wits never stop voicing epigrams and the false wits never stop trying, do not seem to have any connection with the life we know. Situations are designed to be amusing more than probable, characters are exaggerated for comic effect, speeches are carefully patterned and wit intensified. Partly this artificiality results from the heightening of reality characteristic of drama, including Shakespeare's; partly, from the accurate portrayal of a social group in which posing was part of good breeding. (Etherege wrote: "I have been so used to affectation that without the help of the air of the court what is natural cannot touch me. You see what we get by being polished as we call it." [6]) The dramatists did accurately present the surface—the affectations, habits, and amusements—of the social group with whom they were concerned. In the real life of this period, all fashionable people strove for wit like that in the comedies, and some came close to achieving it.

This fact alone would not, however, be enough to make the comedies significant today. The dramatists aimed at, and prided themselves on, a deeper realism, psychological rather than social. They penetrated to the human nature underlying social habits and exposed the pretenses by which people conceal it. Whether we find Restoration comedy realistic depends partly on our agreement with the cynicism of its authors, who (if I may adapt a metaphor from *The Man of Mode*) stripped human nature of its romantic gilding, so that the native brass appeared.[7] To some, the plays appear gross and unduly cynical; but to those who see human nature as more brazen than golden, they are refreshingly realistic. They are certainly tough-minded and honest in the sense that they present selfishness and falsity as they are, stripped of sentimental disguise. Doubtless they reduce sexual relationships to an excessively animalistic level, but they are modern in their scorn for cant and mawkish romance.

The most serious charge that can be leveled at Restoration comedy is that its characters and situations are stereotyped. This failing is common in coterie literature, since a drama restricted in theme and attitudes to the tastes of a limited group is forced to repeat itself. It is true that the comedies could easily degenerate into empty exercises in cleverness, fluent variations on set patterns, like William Congreve's *Old Bachelor*. But the best plays of the best dramatists did not. Not only did the playwrights develop the traditional material in a distinctive way, so that from the stock figure of the fop they drew individuals like the ingenuously complacent Sir Fopling Flutter and the nastily self-absorbed Sparkish. They also *said* something about true and false values, or about man's relationship to woman or to his society.

Of all the Restoration comic dramatists, William Wycherley depended least on the stock situations and attitudes and most on substantial theme and characterization. While his plays flash with the characteristic Restoration wit, they show broader interests and more penetrating social criticism than those of his contemporaries. He invents characters rather than juggling with words; he is concerned with the difference between good and bad more than with the shading between genuine and would-be wit and breeding. He pillories the fop not merely for failing to be a true wit, but for being poisonously selfish. He derides the cuckold not for being a tradesman, but for inviting his own cuckoldom by neglecting or mistreating his wife. He questions the values of a society which required insincerity for success and admired the sexual attitude of a tomcat. He does not laugh at the man who refuses to conform to social expectations but shows the merits of his position. His mature plays, *The Country-Wife* and *The Plain-Dealer*, are free of the complacency to which coterie drama is liable, evident even in a masterpiece like *The Man of Mode*. Wycherley is preoccupied less with shining in society than with behaving decently to one's fellow man. His moral concern deepens his comedy and gives it a substance wanting in the airier creations of his contemporaries.

In this book I have tried to show that Wycherley's plays succeed both as brilliant comedies of wit and as significant comments on society. After sketching the fashionable Restoration milieu in which Wycherley flourished, I have shown how his early plays anticipated his two masterpieces. I have examined in more detail the characters, humor, structure, and satire of Wycherley's major works, *The Country-Wife* and *The Plain-Dealer*. Finally, I have given some account of the latter half of his life, after he stopped writing plays, because this period has not been thoroughly presented elsewhere.

I should like to express my gratitude to the late Professor Richard H. Barker for his generous and perceptive criticism of my manuscript.

KATHARINE M. ROGERS

Brooklyn College of the City University of New York

Contents

Chronology

1641   William Wycherley was born in spring at Clive, near Shrewsbury. Julie, later marquise de Montausier, received *The Garland to Julie,* a collection of tributes from the leading French poets of the day.

1642–1651   The English Civil Wars. In 1642 the theaters were closed by Parliament.

c. 1656   Wycherley went to France, met Madame de Montausier, and was converted to Roman Catholicism.

1660   Charles II was restored to the throne, and soon established two theatrical companies, those of the king and the duke of York. Wycherley returned to England, registered at the public library in Oxford (July), was reconverted to the Church of England. On November 10, 1660, he entered the Inner Temple.

1661   Molière's *The School for Husbands.*

1662   Molière's *The School for Wives.*

1663   Samuel Butler's *Hudibras* (Part I). John Dryden's first play, *The Wild Gallant.*

1664   Wycherley probably left in January for the court of Spain in the suite of the ambassador, Sir Richard Fanshawe, returning to England in February, 1665. George Etherege's first play, *The Comical Revenge.*

1665   June 3: Wycherley probably took part in the great naval victory of the duke of York over Admiral Opdam in the Second Dutch War (1665–67). The Great Plague in London.

1666   Great Fire of London. Molière's *The Misanthrope.*

1667   John Milton's *Paradise Lost.*

1668   Sir Charles Sedley's first play, *The Mulberry Garden.* Thomas Shadwell's first play, *The Sullen Lovers.*

1669   Wycherley's first publication, *Hero and Leander in Burlesque.*

1671   March: the success of Wycherley's first play, *Love in a Wood,* led him to an affair with the duchess of Cleveland and admission to the circle of court wits.

1672   February 6: *The Gentleman Dancing-Master*. June 19: Wycherley commissioned captain-lieutenant in Buckingham's regiment, raised for the Third Dutch War (1672-74). Dryden's *Marriage à la Mode*.

1674   February 28: Wycherley commissioned captain; resigned commission a week later. New Drury Lane Theatre (King's Company) opened.

1675   January 12: *The Country-Wife*. Dryden's *Aureng-Zebe*.

1676   December 11: *The Plain-Dealer*. Etherege's *The Man of Mode*.

1677   Wycherley wrote consolatory verses to Buckingham, imprisoned in the Tower. Dryden's *All for Love*.

1678   Wycherley's catastrophic fever; King Charles sent him to Montpellier to recover his health. Popish Plot. John Bunyan's *The Pilgrim's Progress* (Part I).

1679   Spring: Wycherley returned to England; King Charles offered to make him tutor to the duke of Richmond. Wycherley met Lady Laetitia-Isabella, countess of Drogheda, at Tunbridge Wells. September: Wycherley married Lady Laetitia-Isabella. Lawsuits over her debts and estate.

1681   Lady Laetitia-Isabella died. More lawsuits. Shaftesbury and Buckingham were conspiring against the duke of York. Dryden's *Absalom and Achitophel*.

1682   Wycherley's *Epistles to the King and Duke*. Imprisoned for debt; first, in Newgate; then in the Fleet.

1685   Charles II died, succeeded by James II. December 14: *The Plain-Dealer* was produced at court. King James released Wycherley from prison and gave him a pension (1686). Wycherley reconverted to Roman Catholicism.

1688   James II, forced to abdicate, succeeded by William and Mary. Dryden lost the laureateship; succeeded by Shadwell. Wycherley lost his pension.

1693   William Congreve's first play, *The Old Bachelor*.

1694   John Dennis initiated a correspondence with Wycherley. Thomas Southerne's first play, *The Fatal Marriage*.

1696   Colley Cibber's first play, *Love's Last Shift*. John Vanbrugh's first play, *The Relapse*.

1697   Daniel Wycherley died.

1698   Jeremy Collier's *Short View of the Immorality and Profaneness of the English Stage*. George Farquhar's first play, *Love and a Bottle*.

1700   Dryden died. Congreve's *The Way of the World*.

1702   William III died; succeeded by Anne.

1704   Wycherley's *Miscellany Poems*. Alexander Pope initiated a correspondence with Wycherley in December.

1709   Pope's *Pastorals* and Wycherley's "To my Friend, Mr. Pope on his Pastorals" published in Tonson's *Miscellany*.

1711   Pope's *An Essay on Criticism*. Joseph Addison's and Richard Steele's *The Spectator*.

1714   Anne died; succeeded by George I.

1715   December 20: Wycherley married a young woman. December 31, died.

1728   Lewis Theobald's edition of Wycherley's *Posthumous Works*.

1729   Pope's edition of Wycherley's *Posthumous Works*.

CHAPTER 1

Wycherley's Background

I Shropshire and Angoulême

WILLIAM WYCHERLEY, who was born in the spring of 1641 at Clive Hall near Shrewsbury,[1] was the eldest child of Daniel Wycherley, a self-made squire. Daniel, born to little or no estate, had acquired considerable landed property in the service of the marquis of Winchester, to whom he was High Steward. While the marquis was imprisoned by the Puritans during the Civil War, Daniel had been, in effect, master of his vast estates; he did well for his employer, but he also did so well for himself that he was able to establish himself as a prosperous gentleman. Meanwhile, he had married Bethia Shrimpton, a gentlewoman-companion to the marchioness.

Daniel was a handsome, capable man of genteel manners; but he was ruthless and unscrupulous. He was constantly involved in lawsuits: with the marquis's heir, who charged him with mismanagement of the estate, and with a large number of his neighbors. In 1673, the tenants on Daniel's newly acquired lands sued him for exploiting and oppressing them in various ways, such as charging excessive fees when tenants changed. The suit dragged on until 1677, when the court decreed that the tenants were right. But Daniel Wycherley insisted on new trials by different courts until, with the help of bribes, he finally won his case in 1682. These proceedings cost the tenants three thousand pounds, and Wycherley himself so much that he was forced to sell some of his land.[2] His passion for litigation sometimes conflicted with the other great passion of his life: improving his family's status by amassing more and more land and local influence.

When young William was about fifteen, it was time to finish his education as a gentleman. The elegant court of King Charles I had been supplanted by a bleak Puritan government, many of the nobility were in exile, and the universities were dominated

by Calvinist theologians. It was only natural that Daniel
Wycherley, who had served an ardent Royalist and who had
sent money to Charles II in exile, should decide to have his
son educated abroad. Moreover, a sojourn on the Continent
was then a regular part of a gentleman's education. Usually
the young man would settle first in a French provincial town,
where he would learn to speak the language, to dance and
fence, to carry himself and enter a room. Then he could proceed
to other countries, finishing off with a few months in Paris.
So Daniel Wycherley sent his son to southwestern France, in
or near Angoulême, where he remained for about five years,
presumably under the care of a tutor. There, if not before,
William acquired the basic education in the Latin classics which
was standard for gentlemen in his time and which was to be
evident in his works later.

There also young William became familiar with the French
language, manners, and culture which were an essential part of
good breeding in his day. At Angoulême, he had the good
fortune of being "often admitted to the Conversation of" Julie
d'Angennes, Mme de Montausier, wife of the governor of the
province. The daughter of Mme de Rambouillet, she had grown
up in her mother's salon, where the leaders of Parisian society
and literature had been received on equal terms; conversation
and writing had been cultivated there as elegant arts, and
literary reputations made and lost. She had distinguished herself
for her beauty and wit and was known as "the incomparable
Julie." In 1641, all the famous poets of the era had collaborated
on a collection of poetic tributes to her. Mme de Montausier
gave Wycherley his first glimpse of courtly society, for at
Angoulême she did her best to re-create the atmosphere of a
Parisian salon—constantly entertaining local and Parisian
wits, organizing concerts, balls, and theatrical performances.
Actually—apart from its conspicuous morality—the society which
she cultivated was like that of the Restoration court in fostering
easy, witty social intercourse between men and women, writers
and courtiers.

Mme de Montausier herself—witty, spirited, and assured—
must have revealed to Wycherley how charming a lady could be.
She had many characteristics of the delightful heroines of
Restoration comedy. "Young as he was," Wycherley said in

later life, "he was equally pleas'd with the Beauty of her Mind, and with the Graces of her Person." She "us'd to call him the Little *Hugenot*," [3] and it was probably under her influence that he turned from Protestantism to Roman Catholicism at this time.

Monsieur de Montausier also, it seems, made an impression on Wycherley. A man of competence, courage, and the highest principles, he was equally remarkable for his rigid refusal to compromise or comply with social convention. He prided himself on always telling the truth, regardless of circumstances, even at court. He "was a pattern of virtue and sincerity, if not too cynical in it. He was so far from flattering the king, as all the rest did most abjectly, that he could not hold contradicting him." [4] Molière was to use him as the model for Alceste, the absurdly rigid moralist of *Le Misanthrope;* and Montausier was very much pleased by the representation. Later, Wycherley treated the same theme—a man too sincere to fit into a corrupt society—in his own most passionate play, *The Plain-Dealer.* Perhaps his acquaintance with Montausier first set Wycherley to wonder about how to judge a man whose virtue, while compelling admiration on the one hand, caused him to be harsh, unsociable, and conceited on the other.

Early in 1660, when it became apparent that the Puritan government would fall, Charles II be restored, and English society be reestablished on its old footing, Daniel Wycherley recalled his son from France and sent him to Queen's College, Oxford. There he lived in the house of the head of his college, Thomas Barlow, an able and unscrupulous man who managed to flourish equally under Puritans and Royalist Anglicans. Barlow, a skilled controversialist, soon reconverted Wycherley to Protestantism—not, presumably, a very difficult feat. This conversion seems to have been the only significant effect of Wycherley's stay in Oxford; for, although he registered in the library in July, he never matriculated.

Soon he left the university permanently, to enroll, on November 10, 1660, as a student in the Inner Temple, one of the Inns of Court in London. The Inns of Court, a sort of legal university and the only means of admission to the English Bar, provided a gentleman's education roughly equivalent to that offered by Oxford and Cambridge; and the Inner Temple was, for a young man like Wycherley, much more attractively located. Indeed, Wycherley must have been delighted to leave Oxford for London, since university life of that time would have seemed pedantic and socially crude to a young man polished in France. London, on the other hand, right after the Restoration of King Charles II, offered everything he could have wished for.

The court was not only the center of government, and government preferment, but of fashion and social elegance. London, by far the largest city in England, was predominant in all respects: it was the center of commerce and publishing, the greatest port in England, and the seat of the Royal Society, the most intellectually active group in Great Britain at the time. The upper classes regarded the country as a place of exile, feeling that the only social life worth having was in the parks, assemblies, and taverns of London. "To live like a Philosopher in Suffolk, is to make one's self obscure rather than wise; and forgotten by others, instead of knowing one's self." [5] The only professional theaters in England were in London: the King's Company and the Duke of York's Company, to which Charles had given patents immediately after his restoration.

For Wycherley, then, the Inner Temple afforded convenient lodgings near the mainstream of fashionable life, where his father was willing to support him comfortably. Daniel was undoubtedly delighted to see his son studying the law, that profession by which one could acquire more and more land from one's neighbors.

II *Life in London*

Although the Templars were required to live in the Temple and to participate in moot trials and other legal exercises, all of them were by no means dedicated students of the law. Many were young noblemen and gentry acquiring a smattering of legal knowledge to help them in managing their estates; others used the Temple as a convenient base for enjoying the pleasures of the Town. The Templars constantly appear in contemporary literature as enthusiastic patrons of the theater and as woman chasers. Wycherley, it seems, acquired just enough knowledge of the law to develop an intense distaste for it: his *Plain-Dealer* bristles with satire on meaningless legal rituals and the ways of pettifoggers.

The Temple lay at the eastern edge of "the Town," the world of Restoration comedy and fashionable society alike. Covent Garden, then a district of handsome houses, was "the Heart of the Town," which extended to Whitehall Palace, Westminster Hall, and Saint James's Park in the west. As a Templar, Wycherley presumably kept his legal studies to a minimum and devoted most of his time to watching plays, frequenting the modish coffeehouses and taverns, strolling in Saint James's Park, and picking up news and acquaintances in the galleries of Whitehall. Whitehall Palace, King Charles's principal residence, was a large, rambling group of buildings between the Thames and Saint James's Park, many of which were open to any presentably dressed person. The galleries were usually thronged with people who wanted to hear the latest political rumors, beg a favor from the king as he walked past, meet their acquaintances, or simply see and be seen.

Wycherley's plays are all set in this area. The "Wood" of Wycherley's first play, *Love in a Wood*, is Saint James's Park, where modish people walked on summer evenings. The same play has scenes at the French House (Chateline's), an expensive restaurant in Covent Garden fashionable for its French cuisine and elite clientele; the Old Pall Mall, a broad street near the Park where people delighted in driving their coaches or in walking to admire each other; and the Mulberry Garden, a section of Saint James's Park which provided a dining room, dark paths, and arbors for refreshments and lovemaking. *The Gentleman Dancing-Master* also has a scene at the French House.

The lodgings of Mr. Horner, in *The Country-Wife*, are in Russell Street, which leads out of Covent Garden Square; and there is a scene in the piazza itself. This square, designed by Inigo Jones and surrounded by handsome, arcaded houses and an elegant church, was the pride of London. Characters in the play go to the New Exchange, an arcade a few blocks from the square, to buy some of the fashionable knick-knacks on sale there. In Act III of *The Plain-Dealer*, Wycherley departed a little from this modish milieu by taking his characters to Westminster Hall, where the law courts sat; but even that setting was less than a mile from Covent Garden. Two scenes of *The*

Plain-Dealer are laid at the Cock Tavern, and Olivia's lodgings, where much of the action occurs, are near it.

By 1664 Wycherley must have begun his career as a courtier, for he seems to have been sent to Madrid as attaché to Sir Richard Fanshawe, the newly appointed ambassador to Spain. It is almost certain that William was the "Mr. Wycherley" included in the ambassador's entourage when he presented himself to King Philip IV in June.[6] The ambassador's party, which had left England in January, made a leisurely tour through the chief cities of Spain, being royally entertained everywhere. Probably during this sojourn in Spain Wycherley became acquainted with the plays of Calderón, which were to provide inspiration for his own early work. For a year Wycherley was a "camarado" of Fanshawe, a distinguished translator as well as an experienced diplomat; then, in February, 1665, he returned to England.

Shortly after his return, England declared war on the Dutch (March, 1665); and, along with many young courtiers, Wycherley probably volunteered for naval service. He must have participated in some naval battle, for he wrote a poem "On a Sea Fight, which the Author was in, betwixt the English and Dutch." The poem combines Royalist sentiments with a horrified description of a great and bloody battle, but it provides no details about Wycherley's own role, nor enough about the battle to date the poem definitely.[7] Probably the battle was the duke of York's great victory over Admiral Opdam off Harwich on June 3, 1665, since, in a poem written many years later, Wycherley described the duke's calm courage in battle as if he had himself witnessed it.[8]

It was on the eve of this battle that Charles Sackville, earl of Dorset, wrote his charming, insouciant song "To all you ladies now at land,/ We men at sea indite." Perhaps Wycherley met him at this time. On shipboard Wycherley might have first made acquaintance with a brave and rude sea captain like Manly, the hero of *The Plain-Dealer*. Restoration naval ships, on which professional seamen served and vied with smooth young courtiers, provided a sharp illustration of the contrasting merits of rough worth and social polish.

After a while, like many other Templars, Wycherley tried his hand at witty writing. His first publication, in 1669, was the poem *Hero and Leander in Burlesque*. It was an appropriate form and subject for a fledgeling Restoration wit. Burlesque, a popular genre, had recently been given added impetus by Samuel Butler's brilliant satire on the Puritans, *Hudibras.* Idyllic romance offered an irresistible opportunity; Hero and Leander had already been the subject of several burlesque poems; and Wycherley had probably seen the puppet play in Jonson's *Bartholomew Fair,* which travesties their story. Predictably, Wycherley heavily emphasized the sensuality of the attachment and made Hero, a priestess of Aphrodite in the original, into a procuress. The performance is conventional but amusing, as when Wycherley pokes fun at the artists who strain realism to cover the crucial parts of naked models: "And for the naked Nymphs, of their own Locks/Contrive 'um Aprons, Petticoats, and Smocks." [9] The poem already reveals the obscurity and contorted syntax that were always to clog Wycherley's verse. It does not seem to have made much impression on the Town.

III *The Restoration World*

The society of leisured ladies and gentlemen in London, the class with whom Wycherley now associated and about whom and for whom he wrote his plays, was sensual and uninhibited, brutal and tough-minded, cynical and healthily irreverent, utterly dishonest in public business and private love affairs, but admirably honest in its freedom from self-righteous cant. Idealism had been thoroughly discredited for the young people at Charles II's court. The political and religious absolutes for which men had fought led neither to happiness nor to virtue, only to years of civil war followed by military dictatorship. Moreover, political necessity had caused many of the governing class to abandon loyalty for expediency, and often the turncoats fared better than men who had sacrificed everything for their principles. Finally, any appearance of unusual righteousness was suspect because it was associated with the discredited Puritans, who often behaved as the dramatists charged, covering lewdness or rapacity with pious pretensions. As George Savile, marquis of Halifax, said, "The Hypocrisy of the former Times inclined Men to think they could not shew too great an Aversion to it, and that helped to encourage . . . unbounded liberty of Talking, without the Restraints of Decency which were before observed." [10]

The guiding spirit of Restoration thought was Thomas Hobbes, a materialist who derided abstract principles and proved that in all things men are motivated by naked self-interest. "Every man . . . calleth that which *pleaseth*, and is delightful to himself, *good;* and that *evil*, which *displeaseth* him. . . . Nor is there any such thing as absolute goodness." Hobbes cannot accept "right reason" as a reliable measure, for there is no such thing to be found in nature: "commonly they that call for *right reason* to decide any controversy, do mean their own." Human nature offers "but two imaginable helps" to induce men to keep their agreements: "either a fear of the consequence of breaking their word; or a . . . pride in appearing not to need to break it. This latter is a generosity too rarely found to be presumed on, especially in the pursuers of wealth, command, or sensual pleasure; which are the greatest part of mankind. The passion to be reckoned upon, is fear," of God or of men. "Though the former be the greater power, yet the fear of the latter is commonly the greater fear." [11]

Yet the prosaic morality which Hobbes developed entirely from self-interest does enforce all the important social virtues. Gratitude is a law of nature in order to motivate men to help each other; they would cease to do so if they saw they would derive no benefit from it. Hobbes's morality is completely practical; a man is obligated to return good for good, but not to be meek and dutiful when his neighbors are warring against him.[12] This morality is very much that of Restoration drama such as Wycherley's: transcendent virtue is neither required nor wanted, but people are expected to act according to enlightened self-interest and to do as they have been done by.

The marquis of Halifax agreed with Hobbes that abstract principles are unreal. Any so-called absolute is nothing but "a Nail every body would use to fix that which is good for them: for all Men would have that Principle to be immoveable that serves their use at the time." [13] King Charles, who shared Hobbes's opinion of human motivation, "had a very ill opinion both of men and women; and did not think there was either sincerity or chastity in the world out of principle, but that some had either the one or the other out of humour or vanity." [14]

This withering loss of faith in altruism and moral principles encouraged the naturally selfish to abandon decency in human relationships. There were politicians at court like the character described by Samuel Butler who, considering "that Religion and Morality are but vulgar Errors" and "that all Men are born in the State of War," thought "That Oathes are but Springes to catch Woodcocks withal; and bind none but those, that are too weak and feeble to break them." Such men believed that "Fair Words are all the Civility and Humanity that one Man owes to another." [15] Samuel Pepys complained of the prevailing selfishness of public men—"nobody looking after business, but every man his lust and gain." [16]

The general loss of idealism, which led a few of the courtiers to utter selfishness, encouraged almost universal sensuality and levity. Most of the Restoration court would have sung, with John Wilmot, earl of Rochester, "*Cupid* and *Bacchus* my Saints are." [17] Wine was supposed to induce wit and mirth, and drunkenness seems to have been an essential feature of a sociable evening. Rochester claimed that, as a young man, he had been "five years . . . continually drunk," not visibly under the influence, but never "cool enough to be perfectly master of himself." [18] Inspired by drink, prominent leaders of society and members of Parliament might strip off all their clothes on the balcony of a tavern, preach a blasphemous burlesque sermon, and then "excrementize" over the edge upon the crowd gathered below.[19]

If sophisticated people could not believe in unseen principles, they might as well concentrate on known pleasures—as Sir Charles Sedley advocated when he urged men to enjoy the known goods of "Women, Wine, and Mirth," rather than to aspire toward some dubious future good: the gods, who have placed this knowledge beyond human reach, "laugh to see the Fools afraid,/Of what the Knaves invent." [20]

Though his attitude appears attractively carefree, it could easily lead to a meaningless pursuit of pleasure. For, while the Restoration wits disparaged earnest effort of any kind on the grounds that sophisticated people could perceive its idleness, they failed to recognize that wenching, drinking, and social merriment unrelieved by serious aims are even more empty. In writing, the fashionable dilettantism tended to undermine the sustained effort required to produce literature of value. The court wits wrote little and habitually left their works imperfect. Their satires were formless series of epigrams; their best songs, one or two great stanzas extended with merely adequate ones. Indeed, one sometimes wonders how members of this circle managed to create their three or four plays of sustained brilliance.

The final result of this superficiality was a character like Joseph Addison's futile Will Honeycomb, the superannuated Restoration beau of *The Spectator*. Moreover, those whose business was to rule the country displayed the same frivolity. King Charles, "The easiest Prince and best bred Man alive," [21] was helping his mistress chase a moth around the supper table when, during the Second Dutch War, the Dutch fleet sailed up the Thames to London, towed away the British flagship, and burned the rest of the fleet.[22]

It was an age that questioned all conventions—dedication to business, romantic idealization, righteous professions, moral principles, traditional wisdom—and even suspected individual reason to be futile: "This busie, puzling, stirrer up of doubt,/ That frames deep *Mysteries*, then finds 'em out."[23] If reason was busy idleness, religion was hypocrisy or self-delusion, traditional morality was senseless prescription,[24] the Restoration wit was left with nothing to believe in. Sense alone cannot provide an adequate reason for living, nor could Hobbes's practical teachings. One result of this withering doubt was the self-destructive dissipation of a life like Rochester's. Another was the inadequacy of the ideal characters in Restoration drama. The dramatists, unable to believe in ideals but feeling a need for them, could not create noble characters more satisfying than the absurdly unreal protagonists of heroic drama or the implausible Fidelia of Wycherley's own *Plain-Dealer*.

On the other hand, Restoration cynicism encouraged a healthy contempt for cant and self-delusion. The cynicism which destroyed faith or justified low selfishness could also deflate pious pretensions. It was just as devastating to self-righteousness, hypocrisy, and sentimentality as it was to lofty idealism. To some extent the apparent increase of sin after the Restoration was, as the dramatists claimed, merely an abandonment of hypocrisy. But the reaction against Puritan hypocrisy often went too far: just as the Puritans had often mistaken sanctimonious pretense for virtue, the Restoration rakes often mistook shocking words and behavior for manly honesty.[25]

The Restoration court was most shocking, of course, in its sexual behavior. King Charles had a stable of mistresses who flaunted themselves in society and who were abjectly flattered by English courtiers and foreign ambassadors alike. In 1663 the king was "besotted upon Mrs. Stewart . . . gets into corners, and will be with her half an hour together kissing her to the observation of all the world; and she now stays by herself, and expects it, as my Lady Castlemaine did use to do; to whom the King . . . is still kind." [26] So kind was he that Lady Castlemaine (Barbara Palmer, later the duchess of Cleveland) appeared at a court play in jewels estimated "at 40000 pounds & more: & far out shining the Queene."[27] King Charles's "Inclinations to Love were the Effects of Health, and a good Constitution, with as little mixture of the *Seraphick* part as ever Man had." He did not much object to unfaithfulness in his mistresses because, "where mere *Nature* is the Motive, it is possible for a Man to think righter than the common opinion, and to argue, that a Rival taketh away nothing but the Heart, and leaveth all the rest."[28]

The king's example was followed by most of his court, so much so that an important officer of the government could be seriously advised to keep a whore because "he was ill looked upon for want of doing so."[29] If the courtiers lived chaste, it was only for want of a suitable partner. As Dorset put it, at the end of a highly obscene letter to his friend Etherege, "For want of bouncing bona roba / Lasciva est nobis pagina vita proba."[30] The naughtiness and the witty misapplication of a Classical verse (from Martial's *Epigrams*, I, 4) are equally typical of a Restoration courtier.

Speech, too, was incredibly obscene. The king himself "was apter to make *broad Allusions* upon anything that gave the least occasion, than was altogether suitable with the very Good-breeding he shewed in most other things." [31] The libels which circulated constantly about the Town—passed from hand to hand in taverns, coffeehouses, and the galleries of Whitehall because it was too dangerous to publish them—attacked the leaders of government, court ladies, the royal mistresses, and even the king with unrestrained coarseness.

For example, Dorset, a generous, responsible man noted for his good nature and one of the worthiest of Restoration courtiers, wrote a poem representing the ladies of the court as competing for succession to the duchess of Portsmouth's place as chief mistress. The duchess of Richmond is rejected because she has miscarried so often ("a c——t so us'd to puke / Could never bear a booby duke," a royal bastard); Jane Middleton, because she has supported her family on the generosity of her lovers, and besides her armpits and toes stink; her daughter Jane, because she has had a lesbian affair with Lady Harvey, which is incestuous too, because she is really the illegitimate daughter of Lady Harvey's brother; and so forth.[32]

All these ladies were the cream of contemporary society. The charges are appalling even if, as one hopes, they show the extent to which libel, rather than vice, could go at the Restoration court. No one had mawkish scruples about wounding the fair sex. If a courtier was slighted by a lady, especially if she favored a rival of his, he immediately cast about for a suitable means of revenge, exposing her secret love affairs if possible, otherwise circulating lampoons on her. And the ladies often retaliated with counter-lampoons of equal scurrility.

Manners were free to the point of coarseness, even when there was no sexual misbehavior. A contemporary writer on etiquette found it necessary to admonish young gentlemen not to put their hands into ladies' bosoms, to kiss them by surprise, or to seize their ribbons to put in their hats; "You must be very familiar to use them at this rate." On a visit to a person of superior rank, "You must forbear hawking and spitting as much as you can," or at least—if the room is clean—refrain from spitting on the floor.[33] Pepys was once accidentally spat upon in the theater; but, since the spitter was an unusually pretty lady, he "was not troubled at it at all." He described a merry—and innocent—evening during which the various ladies present took turns flinging him down backward on the bed, throwing themselves down on top of him.[34]

Restoration writers regularly equated love with sensual attraction and therefore expected it to be transitory. They dismissed platonic love as a fatuous fantasy, romantic idealization as a fiction, and chastity as an empty convention. They thought of love as a game in which a man and a woman, meeting on equal terms, vied for supremacy; whoever remained faithful after the other lost interest had lost the game. The man tried to persuade the woman to sleep with him; the woman, to attract the man's attention and retain it, without sleeping with him, until he proposed marriage. The woman wanted marriage because it was her only acceptable social role; the man resisted it because it restrained him from following nature's call in sexual matters. No one but a fool fell blindly in love; intelligent people took care to secure mates whom they could live with comfortably, that being all that a sensible person could expect from marriage.

The gentlemen's attempts to seduce and abandon women and their abusive attacks on them when an affair terminated[35] indicate a sadistic streak in the fashionable Restoration attitude toward love. A view of love which excludes idealism and altruism is not only base but unrealistic. The shallow inadequacy of the wits' attitude is revealed by the opinion, voiced by Dryden but typical of the whole group, that Ovid was the most profound authority on the subject: "no man . . . has ever treated the passion of love with so much delicacy . . . or searched into the nature of it more philosophically than he."[36]

On the other hand, much of what the Restoration poets scornfully brush away *is* cant. If a man desires a woman simply for sexual gratification, why should he swathe his feelings in romantic sentiments? If a woman lets a notorious rake seduce her, why should there be melodramatic talk of ruin or maudlin sentiment about broken hearts when he leaves? If a woman is vicious, why should not a man say so, unhampered by the fiction that she is too fragile to attack? The self-aware courtship of a Restoration comedy couple approaching marriage is quite as true a picture of the sexual relationship as the blind self-surrender of a romantic couple in love.

Moreover, the Restoration wits' presentation of love and marriage must be evaluated in terms of the social practices of their time. Although marriage was nominally a sacred contract, there was actually little sanctity about it. Marrying for love was regarded as a notable folly, and parents generally arranged marriages, often for mercenary motives. Halifax, an unusually devoted and conscientious father, told his daughter not only that she should accept the husband her family chose for her but that this man might well be a whoremaster, a drunkard, a fool, or a sadist.[37] He haggled for months over a marriage between his son and the duke of Newcastle's daughter because he wanted fifteen thousand pounds ready cash with the girl, while her father would only offer sixty thousand pounds at his death or second marriage. All this time Newcastle had not seen the prospective bridegroom, although he did insist on it before a definite arrangement was made, having "heard he was very debauched."[38]

Religious writers of the time used pious appeals as a means for keeping women in subjection, insisting that it was a woman's Christian duty to submit completely to her male relatives. The author of *The Ladies Calling*, a popular manual of female conduct, conceded that a virgin might refuse a suitor but warned her against expressing a preference for anyone, lest she be suspected of "somwhat too warm desires": "'tis most agreeable to the virgin modesty . . . [to] make marriage an act rather of their obedience than their choise." If a woman's husband mistreats her, she must be like the unprotesting lamb under the knife, which moves one to pity, rather than the recalcitrant swine.[39]

Of course the Restoration wits were irresponsibly scornful of the marriage bond—but they also saw that a marriage based on unenlightened self-interest was not sacred; and they did not hide exploitation under smug domestic pieties. Wycherley was not being gratuitously coarse when he stated that Mr. Pinchwife's motive for marriage was to have a whore to himself: he was exposing Pinchwife's selfishness for what it was, instead of letting it hide under a respected sacrament. The court wits were motivated partly by the iconoclasm of their class, an urge to break down the bourgeois ideals of the sanctity of marriage and the subjection of women, which the Puritans had so rigorously insisted upon. But partly theirs was an honest desire to see things as they are and to make morality sensible by stripping it of deception. They saw that women are intelligent beings capable of acting independently and defending themselves; they recognized that it was not right to claim freedom for themselves and require women to be meek and submissive.

Accordingly, the Restoration playwrights consistently maintain that girls should be permitted to go about freely and "take their innocent Diversion"; for, if they are virtuous, they will not abuse their freedom; and, if they are vicious, they cannot be restrained anyway. Sedley's *The Mulberry Garden* makes this point explicitly, and it is implicit in all the best Restoration comedies. His four lively heroines adeptly play a love game with the gentlemen they have chosen, teasing them because "it gives 'um an Opinion of our wit; and is consequently a Spur to theirs."[40]

It appears that the feminine ideal and the social relationships between the sexes which Restoration comedy presents did reflect actuality in upper-class Restoration circles. Although women were legally subject to their husbands, they seem to have moved freely at Charles's court, taking part in social activities and playing the love game with the men. Etherege, when on duty as a diplomat in Ratisbon, complained bitterly of the contrast between the freedom of London and the impediments to social intercourse with the German ladies: Ratisbon was so censorious that a gentleman and a lady seen playing cards together were assumed to be having an affair, and "an innocent Piece of Gallantry" was construed as "a criminal Correspondence."[41] The feminine ideal of the Restoration was no meek lamb, but a witty woman who could hold her own with a man and effect her wishes in the choice of a mate. Even Halifax told his daughter that wit and virtue were equally necessary to a woman: separated, "the first is so empty, and the other so faint, that they scarce have right to be commended."[42]

The most engaging feature of the age was its wit—not only what it displayed, but the unprecedented value it placed on wit. King Charles told anecdotes so superlatively well that his company was sought even by "those who had no other Design than to be merry with him."[43] The society that revelled in Restoration comedy must have been clever and quick witted. Dryden attributed the brilliant portraits of ladies and gentlemen in comedy to the increased cultivation of wit in the upper classes and to the freer conversation between courtiers and playwrights.[44] Etherege and Wycherley, the two most gifted dramatists of the time, were personal friends of the king; and both Dryden and Shadwell were well acquainted in court circles, although they were not quite accepted as equals. At one period Dorset would appear at court only "once in three months, for he drinks ale with Shadwell and Mr. Harris [an actor] at the Duke's house [theater] all day long."[45]

At no other time in history was wit so emphasized as a necessary social qualification for both sexes. Richard Steele described the intellectual atmosphere at Will's Coffee-House in the Restoration as it contrasted to that of his own day: "where you used to see songs, epigrams, and satires in the hands of every man you met, you have now only a pack of cards; and instead of cavils about the turn of the expression, the elegance of the style, and the like, the learned now dispute about the truth of the game."[46] Although Alexander Pope might sneer at "The mob of gentlemen who wrote with ease,"[47] it was something that every man of fashion tried to be an author and that so many of them wrote so well. It must be admitted that, since no one could be socially acceptable who was not a wit, people vainly strove for wit who were incapable of anything beyond farfetched similes, malicious sneers, and inane verses. The fops who infest the comedies were drawn directly from the social scene.

Sometimes this extreme emphasis on wit led to the heartless belief that a wit could and should make fun of anything that offered the least room for a jest. Anthony Hamilton's *Memoirs of the Comte de Gramont* detail an endless series of cruel practical jokes, unconvincingly attributed to the desire to reform vanity or folly. "In our vertuous Age," wrote a contemporary poet, "Not only every wit, Lampoons his brother, / But men are all burlesque to one another."[48]

But the more mature courtiers, men like Wycherley, saw that it was only the false wit who delighted in universal derision. Many of the leaders of taste, including Wycherley, Dorset, and King Charles himself, were conspicuous for their good nature. King Charles, who "could not think God would make a man miserable only for taking a little pleasure out of the way,"[49] was kind and forgiving. If the wits made light of their duties to God, they often showed loyalty and generosity to their fellow men.

Never had the governing classes been so close to the theater as in the Restoration, when fashionable people went to plays almost daily during the season. King Charles often gave money and clothes to make plays magnificent and took a personal interest in the actors (as well as the actresses). When George Villiers, duke of Buckingham, produced his *Rehearsal,* a lampoon on heroic plays with particular emphasis on Dryden's, he spent hours coaching John Lacy to mimic Dryden. He also made a point of bringing Dryden with him to the play and of watching him squirm with mortification during the performance.

At the revival of Jonson's *Catiline* on December 18, 1668 (for which, incidentally, the king gave the theater five hundred pounds for new costumes), Elizabeth Corey was to play Sempronia, a ridiculous mannish she-politician. The duchess of Cleveland bribed Mrs. Corey to mimic Lady Elizabeth Harvey, an eccentric and officiously political lady prominent at court. The audience was convulsed with laughter, but Lady Harvey succeeded in getting the actress imprisoned. Immediately the duchess made the king release her and order her "to act it again, worse than ever," when he himself was present in the royal box. Thereupon Lady Harvey "provided people to hiss her and fling oranges at her."[50] The episode shows not only the general lack of inhibitions but the close connection between court and theater and the intimacy of a world in which mimicry of a court lady would be immediately recognized by the audience in a public theater.

To John Milton, the court wits were "the Sons / Of *Belial,* flown with insolence and wine." (Graceful Belial, "To vice industrious" but uninterested in nobler deeds, was the lewdest spirit that fell.)[51] To John Bunyan, the London world was a Vanity Fair, populated by "fools, apes, knaves," where everything was for sale.[52] But, for Wycherley at twenty, it was a world of gaiety, brilliance, fashion, prestige, excitement; it offered the only good life.

CHAPTER 2

The Rise to Fame

I *Love in a Wood*

AFTER *Hero and Leander* (1669), Wycherley turned to a more congenial form, the drama. His *Love in a Wood, or, St. James's Park* (1671) develops conventional subject matter with a vigor and humor already distinctive. By 1671, Restoration comedy of manners had taken shape, although none of its masterpieces had yet been written. The cast of a typical comedy included pairs of modish lovers, one pair at least engaged in a witty love game; an elderly widow pretending to starched virtue but actually disgracefully eager to catch a man; one or two hypocritical Puritan citizens; a few loose women; and a fop, or would-be wit. The scene was London; the action, the mating of the appropriate couples, with the outwitting of the fools; the matter, chiefly, witty dialogue.

Wycherley produced a thoroughly amusing example of this genre. In *Love in a Wood*, Ranger, a typical Restoration rake, is trying to elude his cousin Lydia because he does not want to get married, especially not to a woman whom he undervalues because she already loves him. He prefers to pursue Christina, Valentine's fiancée, mainly because she is engaged to another man. Fortunately, Lydia has enough wit and spirit to capture Ranger anyway. He learns the falsity of his complacent masculine assumption that "Women are poor credulous Creatures, easily deceived" by being made to look foolish by both the young ladies in the play; and he finally admits: "*Lydia*, triumph . . . of Intrigues, honourable or dishonourable, and all sorts of rambling, I take my leave; when we are giddy, 'tis time to stand still."[1]

Meanwhile, Lady Flippant, an elderly widow in pursuit of a husband and an income, is scheming to marry Dapperwit, the fop of the play, or—failing him—Sir Simon Addleplot, the dupe, who plots to marry Lady Flippant only if he can not win the more appetizing Martha, daughter of Lady Flippant's brother, the usurer Gripe. Dapperwit, however, elopes with Martha, who turns out to be not so desirable a match because she is six months' pregnant. Gripe, to spite his daughter, marries his wench, Lucy, in hopes of begetting other children to succeed to his fortune. Lady Flippant is left with Addleplot; and each, secretly destitute, marries the other for his supposed fortune.

Although Wycherley took his inspiration from Calderón's *Mañanas de abril y mayo*, his own comedy is completely different from Calderón's in tone and effect. From Calderón he took only the extravagantly jealous Valentine and his saintly fiancée Christina, and they are obviously out of keeping with the rest of the play. Valentine's jealousy is as selfish and neurotically stupid as Mr. Pinchwife's in *The Country-Wife*, and should be likewise punished; yet Wycherley rewards him with a loving wife. When Christina locks herself in her room for a month while Valentine must be out of the country, or persists in believing him "worthy the love of a Princess . . . good as Angels," she appears fatuous in a realistic comedy peopled by down-to-earth characters who want to gratify themselves and to take revenge for injuries.[2] Like most of his contemporary dramatists, Wycherley had not yet realized that sentimental heroics did not belong in the Restoration comedy of manners.

Dapperwit, the would-be wit, is at the same time less clever than the true wits and more conceited about his "parts." He is so proud of his similes that he pauses to complete one while he is eloping with Martha, when her hostile father may interrupt them at any moment. He would willingly sacrifice mistress or friend to his jest, inane as it inevitably is. Just as Dapperwit contrasts with the true wits, he also contrasts with the dullards—Sir Simon Addleplot, who wistfully admires him, and the Puritan Gripe, who hates a wit more than anything. Dapperwit is convinced that "Wit is lost upon a silly weak woman," but actually Lydia can make a fool of him without even trying. When they meet at night in Saint James's Park, she immediately recognizes him, though he does not know her; and she proceeds to exhaust his small stock of witty invention:

Dapperwit: It will not be morning, dear Madam, till you pull off your mask; that I think was brisk—*[Aside*
Lydia: Indeed, dear Sir, my face would frighten back the Sun.

37

Dapperwit: With glories, more radient than his own; I keep up with
her I think. *[Aside*
But, when Lydia tells him he cannot read his verses now for
want of light, he is at a loss about what to answer:
Dapperwit: I dare not make use again of the lustre of her face:
[Aside] I'll wait upon you home then, Madam.

Lydia goes on to draw out Dapperwit on the different types of wit
—the courtier, the coffeehouse politician, and so forth—which
leads to his own claim to be the only true wit, the critic, whose
"wit lies in damming all but himself."[3] The irony lies not only
in Dapperwit's incapacity to attain his ideal but in the falsity
of an ideal which makes wit inconsistent with good nature and
loyal friendship. The comprehensive catalogue of wits is Wycherley's mockery of a society in which everybody aspired to be
a wit.

Wycherley's strong humor comes out particularly in his presentation of the hypocrites, the Puritan Gripe and Lady Flippant.
Gripe, though plainly derived from Jonson's Puritans, is very
funny as he is torn between lechery and greed or as he manages
to talk self-righteously even when caught in the most disgraceful
situations. Entering the room of a poverty-stricken wench whom
he plans to make his mistress, he intones, "Peace, Plenty, and
Pastime be within these Walls." He is echoing a well-known
contemporary blessing, "Peace be within thy walls, and pros-
perity within thy palaces"; the harmoniously alliterative "pastime" slips in to reveal what is actually on Gripe's mind. The
emptiness of his use of "plenty" is shown by his subsequent
stinginess, which he unctuously justifies on the grounds that
"Temperance is the nurse of Chastity." Eventually, when the
girl accuses him of raping her and insists on a five-hundred
pound bribe for silence, he agrees on the grounds that "My
enemies are many, and I shall be [as] a scandal to the Faithful,
as a laughing-stock to the wicked; go, prepare your Engines for
my Persecution."[4]

Lady Flippant, who declaims against marriage while avidly
pursuing every male in sight, is a stock type who is vitalized
by Wycherley's distinctive satiric force. Wycherley made good
use in this play of what was to be one of his most successful
comic and satiric devices: speech of double meaning through
which a hypocrite unwittingly reveals the truth about himself.

Lady Flippant, pretending intense reluctance to accompany Lydia to Saint James's Park at night, exclaims: "I hope, Madam, the fellows do not make honourable Love here, do they? I abominate honourable Love, upon my Honour."[5] She is more truthful than she realizes, for she does in fact abominate honorable love, wanting only dishonorable affairs.

Even in this first play there are signs of the moral awareness which was to distinguish Wycherley among his contemporaries. While men like Etherege and Rochester seemed to measure every human motive and action on an intellectual scale alone, Wycherley was genuinely concerned about kindness, loyalty, and fair dealing. The characters he derides are morally as well as mentally deficient. While the average fop in Restoration drama is harmlessly narcissistic, Wycherley's fops are shown to be odiously selfish and unprincipled: immediately on getting an opportunity, Dapperwit begins to backbite his supposed friends.

Lady Flippant's railing against men and marriage is not just a foolish attempt to cover her real desires: it reveals her sadistic, exploitative attitude toward men. She is consistently nasty to Sir Simon, even though she is thinking of marrying him; it never occurs to her that she should give kindness or loyalty to a man. If she fails to "whedle, jilt, trace, discover, countermine, undermine, and blow up the stinking fellows," it is only because of her own ineptitude. Eager as she is for marriage, she "never did so mean a thing, as really to love any" man, and especially would never be "so ill bred, as to love a Husband"; she assumes that one is only nice to a man to get presents from him, and she would rather be nice to a lover than to a husband.[6] Wycherley not only ridicules her transparent attempts to cover lust with prudery but also condemns her pursuit of men for lust and money when she has no regard at all for the men themselves. He detested such mercenary nymphomaniacs, whom he was to attack more violently in his later characters of Lady Fidget and Olivia.

Wycherley's moral concern appears also in the character of Vincent, who is contrasted with his more typical friend Ranger. Vincent, with "grave parts, and manly wit," [7] is less complaisant than Ranger; he cannot stand Dapperwit's attempts at cleverness and constantly tries to drive him away with insults. He is more punctiliously loyal, for he refuses to take part in miscellaneous detraction, lest he unwittingly malign a friend. Although he has amours, he is not, like Ranger, totally irresponsible in his dealings with women. Realizing that Christina is honorable (as her fiancé, Valentine, has not the sense to do), he takes great pains to clear her good name. His loyalty, sincerity, and distaste for social pliability suggest Wycherley's admiration for these qualities and make Vincent a shadowy precursor of the author's most famous character, Manly of *The Plain-Dealer* (1676).

Love in a Wood appears to be merely a brisk presentation of the problems of several pairs of lovers who are separated by obstacles and misunderstandings—"in a wood" meant "in confusion" or "perplexed"—and ultimately united. But there is already a suggestion that there are reasons why love is in a wood—social and psychological reasons, not just the conventions of romantic comedy. It is not hostile fortune that keeps the lovers apart, but Ranger's compulsive inconstancy, Valentine's senseless and selfish jealousy, and a generally self-seeking and mercenary attitude toward sexual relationships. The opening line of the play—Lady Flippant's "Not a Husband to be had for mony"—reveals not only her personal attitude toward marriage but that of her whole society. The line shocks by its incongruity, but the contemporary marriages of convenience bore out its truth: money was the only reliable quality for getting a husband or a wife. The widow's methods for getting a husband, however ludicrous in terms of her unattractiveness, were standard ones.

The physical confusion of the lovers in the last act, as the two young couples mistake each other's identity in the dark, is a psychological confusion as well—as is shown when Vincent introduces evidence of Christina's innocence to Valentine with the speech, "now I am prepar'd to lead you out of the dark." The final couplet—Ranger's "The end of Marriage, now is liberty,/ And two are bound—to set each other free" [8] is ambiguous, for it may merely express the conventional Restoration cynicism that marriage makes it easier for people to have affairs with others. But an interpretation more appropriate to the plot and the moral of the play is that the four young people, enabled to marry because cured of their wrong attitudes toward sex and love, are only now psychologically free to have a good relationship with a member of the opposite sex.

Although *Love in a Wood* is not one of the masterpieces of Restoration drama, it is a funny and spirited play. The characters are conventional, but well marked and amusing. Unlike the empty, conscienceless plays of such contemporaries as Edward Ravenscroft and Aphra Behn, which aimed merely at eliciting laughs through sexual misunderstandings, *Love in a Wood* demonstrates a moral point of view; for Wycherley reforms or punishes selfish and heartless behavior. He makes Ranger look ridiculous before allowing him to marry Lydia; and he disappoints Sir Simon, Lady Flippant, and Dapperwit, who are alike devoid of consideration for others and determined to marry for money.

Love in a Wood, produced at the Theatre Royal in Bridges Street in March, 1671, was a triumphant success. The theater was small and intimate by American, twentieth-century standards, for five hundred spectators represented a moderately profitable house and one thousand a full one.[9] Although the picture-frame stage had come into use with the Restoration, most of the action took place on the forestage, which projected farther forward than in modern theaters. There were two permanent doors on either side of the forestage, through which the actors generally made their exits and entrances. Scenery (all behind the proscenium arch) consisted of movable flats, which, for comedies, were painted realistically with the appropriate scenes of contemporary London.

The actors and actresses (the latter an innovation of the Restoration) were, by all accounts, particularly competent. The original cast of *Love in a Wood* included Charles Hart, who could have taught "any King on earth how to Comport himself" in his tragic roles and equally "shone in the gay gentlemen," as Ranger; Michael Mohun, a "little Man of Mettle" and great versatility, as Dapperwit; and two excellent comic actresses, Mary Knepp and Elizabeth Corey, as Lady Flippant and the Puritan procuress Mrs. Joyner, respectively. Betty Boutell, who played Christina, was short and pretty, with a good figure, an appealing manner, and "a childish look."[10] Her apparent naïveté helped her, later, to create the role of Margery Pinchwife; her wistful manner and good figure, the "breeches part" of Fidelia.

The theater audience was divided among pit, box, and gallery. The pit, immediately before and around the forestage and furnished with backless benches, was occupied by men-about-town—young courtiers, idle gentlemen, law students—by a few ladies and by many prostitutes, who found the theater a profitable place to ply their trade. They made a disorderly group, fighting and flirting, talking loudly, and making a spectacle of themselves in competition with the show on stage. Pepys describes Sir Charles Sedley at a dull play: "he did at every line take notice of the dullness of the poet and badness of the action, that most pertinently; which I was mightily taken with." [11] Indeed, the play had to be sparkling and the actors accomplished to hold the attention of such an audience! On the other hand, the audience must have been quick witted as well as restless, or it could never have followed the elaborate repartee of Restoration comedy.

The critics in the pit, who included both true wits and carping pretenders like Dapperwit, usually determined the fate of a play. Pepys, at the premiere of Etherege's *She Would if she Could,* described Buckingham, Dorset, Sedley, and Etherege sitting together in the pit. He listened to Etherege "mightily find fault with the actors . . . while all the rest did, through the whole pit, blame the play as a silly, dull thing." [12] In this case the pit was wrong, but often a few admired wits could sway the pit, and hence the general public, in favor of a deserving play. John Dennis attributed the superiority of Restoration drama to that of his own time, the early eighteenth century, to the influence of such critics.[13] A small, homogeneous audience could be directed by a few recognized leaders of taste, who thus, if discerning, could exercise a good influence on the public drama.

The galleries, the cheapest part of the theater, were occupied by poorer and less fashionable people: country cousins, such citizens and their wives who did not recoil from the theater as a nursery of vice, apprentices, servants, and the poorer prostitutes. The boxes, flanking the Royal Box—which directly faced the stage and was frequently occupied by the king himself, his family, or his mistresses—were for aristocrats, chiefly ladies. They were conveniently located so that a gentleman who stood in the pit could easily converse, during the intermissions or the play itself, with a lady seated in a box.

A very important lady attended *Love in a Wood* two days in succession—Barbara Palmer, duchess of Cleveland.[14] Perhaps the most beautiful woman of her day, with blazing blue eyes and

dark auburn hair, she had been the king's undisputed reigning
mistress for over eight years. She was then about thirty, Wycherley's own age. Although she had by this time lost place to the
more refined duchess of Portsmouth, she still exerted considerable
influence as a result of her extraordinary beauty, imperious
temper—in her rages she "bore less resemblance to Medea . . .
than to Medea's yoke of dragons" [15]—and five royal children.
As lustful as her royal master himself, she had embarked on the
series of miscellaneous liaisons which occupied her from the
time that she had lost her position as reigning mistress. She was
delighted with the play, particularly with a song by Lady Flippant which ended "Great Wits, and great Braves, / Have always
a Punk to their Mother." [16]

Moreover, the author of the play was strikingly handsome as
well as witty. Wycherley was tall and strongly built; and he
possessed piercing, lively eyes; a straight, prominent nose; sensual, shapely lips; an expression of elegant, haughty virility; and
the bearing of a nobleman.[17] He was undoubtedly in the audience
to observe the reception of his play, and it would have been easy
for the duchess to get him pointed out to her. In any case, shortly
thereafter, as Wycherley was driving down Pall Mall, the duchess,
passing him in her chariot, thrust her body half out of the window and screamed, "You, Wycherley, you are the Son of a
Whore!," at the same time laughing heartily. Naturally taken
aback at first, Wycherley soon caught the reference to his own
song. When he overtook the lady, he said, "Madam, you have
been pleased to bestow a Title on me which generally belongs
to the Fortunate. Will your Ladyship be at the Play to-Night?"
After an exchange of artful gallantry, they arranged to meet at
the theater that night (actually at three or four in the after-
noon, when the plays regularly began). She appeared in the first
row of the king's box, with Wycherley in the pit underneath,
whence "he entertained her during the whole Play." [18]

Thus opened an affair which, though presumably shortlived
(Wycherley was soon succeeded by Jack Churchill, the future
duke of Marlborough), helped to introduce Wycherley to the
most desirable of Restoration social circles, that of the court wits
who were King Charles's favored companions. Wycherley acknowledged his obligations to the duchess when he dedicated

Love in a Wood to her on its publication at the end of the year. The dedication is gracefully done, wittily self-deprecating and relatively honest by Restoration standards: Wycherley emphasized the lady's indisputable beauty, and he barely alluded to her dubious intellectual and moral virtues. It is a manly and self-respecting dedication compared to most of the period, which tended to be utterly servile. (In a dedication to Dorset, Dryden said that his satires owed all their merit to being copies of Dorset's.)[19] Nevertheless, Wycherley seems to have been unhappy about dedications, so often used to solicit money obsequiously; for *The Gentleman Dancing-Master* and *The Country-Wife* have none; *The Plain-Dealer* and *Miscellany Poems,* burlesque ones.

II *Acceptance by the Court Wits*

Even without the duchess of Cleveland's help, however, so eminently presentable an author would undoubtedly have made his way into the circle of court wits, as another gentleman, Etherege, had done after the success of his first play seven years before. This group of clever and charming, if debauched and disorderly, young men included the earl of Rochester, a gifted poet with the face of a fallen angel, who was so charming that the king repeatedly forgave him even for lampoons on the royal person and mistresses. Another member was the pathologically changeable duke of Buckingham, a man of enormous gifts who managed to dissipate them almost as completely as he did his equally enormous fortune. He was, by all accounts, justly characterized by Dryden as a man who, "in the course of one revolving Moon,"

> Was Chymist, Fidler, States-man, and Buffoon;
> Then all for Women, Painting, Rhiming, Drinking,
> Besides ten thousand Freaks that died in thinking.
> Blest Madman, who coud every hour employ,
> With something New to wish, or to enjoy!
> Railing and praising were his usual Theams;
> And both (to shew his Judgment) in Extreams.[20]

But, fickle and self-indulgent as he was, Buckingham consistently fought for religious liberty at a time when tolerance was seldom found among the more sober members of society. "Nothing can be more anti-christian," he wrote, "nor more contrary to sense and reason, than to trouble and molest our fellow christians, because they cannot be exactly of our minds in all the things relating to the worship of God." [21]

Little Sedley was a brilliant conversationalist, of whom Etherege wrote: "Few of our plays can boast of more wit than I've heard him speak at a supper." [22] He and Dorset ("the grace of Courts, the Muses' pride, / Patron of arts, and judge of Nature") [23] were minor writers capable of producing exquisite songs, who in later life took a responsible role in government. John Sheffield, earl of Mulgrave, whom Rochester called "My Lord All-Pride," ranked as a court wit in spite of his conceit and humorless pomposity. (He thought Dryden's poems "sometimes" deserved as much applause as his own.) [24]

This group, with three or four others, led public taste in plays and in other fashionable literature; got together for convivial evenings devoted to literary criticism and to the composition of satiric poems, as well as to drink and riot; and often joined the king himself at the frequent suppers, usually in the rooms of one of the royal mistresses, where he enjoyed himself with the company he most liked. Dryden gives an only slightly idealized picture of the wits' "genial nights" in a dedication to Sedley: "Our discourse is neither too serious, nor too light, but always pleasant, and for the most part instructive: the raillery neither too sharp upon the present, nor too censorious on the absent; and the cups only such as will raise the conversation of the night, without disturbing the business of the morrow." He goes on to say that he has never met at Sedley's such impious wits as the scandalized prigs describe, "but have often heard much better reasoning at your table, than I have encountered in their books. The wits they describe are the fops we banish: for blasphemy and atheism, if they were neither sin nor ill manners, are subjects so very common, and worn so threadbare." [25] It seems unlikely that the wits worried about the sin of blasphemy, but they would indeed have shunned a subject that was trite.

While Wycherley was having his affair with the duchess of Cleveland, he made the acquaintance of Buckingham, her cousin. Possibly because Buckingham was one of the few men she had refused, more likely because he was jealous of her influence over the king, whom he wanted to control himself, Buckingham resolved to ruin her by exposing her with her lover—at this time, as it happened, Wycherley; and he was characteristically oblivious to the probable effects on Wycherley. Now Wycherley, a young man who felt the need of a handsome income and had no financial resources except grudging supplies from his father, depended on preferment at court for position and money. And, of course, if the king were infuriated against him, there would be no possibility of a court career.

Since, by good fortune, Wycherley was already personally acquainted with Buckingham's friends Rochester and Sedley, he asked them to remonstrate with the duke against ruining a man whom he did not even know. Accordingly, two or three nights later, they brought Wycherley to have supper with Buckingham; and Wycherley, who took pains to exert himself for the occasion, so charmed his host "that he cry'd out in a Transport, By G——, my Cousin is in the right of it! and from that very Moment made a Friend of a Man whom he believed his happy Rival." Not only did Buckingham make a friend of Wycherley, but he helped him more tangibly: being Master of the Horse, he appointed Wycherley an equerry of the royal household.[26] The post was largely a sinecure, involving only occasional attendance on the king, and carried an income which he was no doubt very grateful to receive. In addition, King Charles sometimes gave him a hundred pounds.[27]

By this time, Wycherley was a fully accepted member of the court wits, having the requisite combination of wit, in writing and conversation, and social attractiveness. King Charles "often chose him for a Companion at his leisure Hours."[28] Other successful playwrights, Dryden and Thomas Shadwell, mingled with the wits socially and liked to think of themselves as members of the circle; but they were often patronized as inferiors, partly because they wrote for money. In "An Allusion to Horace, The Tenth Satyr of the First Book" (written in 1675 or 1676), Rochester wrote of Dryden from the standpoint of an aristocratic arbiter of wit passing judgment on a mere practitioner; but no such insinuation appears in his remarks about Wycherley. Rochester declared that the only modern writers who had once touched upon "true *Comedy*" were "hasty *Shadwel,* and slow *Wicherley,*" who

> . . . earnes hard what e're he gains,
> He wants no judgment, nor he spares no pains;
> He frequently excells, and at the least,
> Makes fewer faults, than any of the best.

The praise is measured to an ungenerous degree, but is relatively high, for Rochester, and not at all patronizing. For some reason, Wycherley was nettled at the epithet "slow," perhaps because he shared the silly contemporary opinion that only a dull plodder took pains over anything. He seems to have made a point of insisting that he wrote "with as much Ease and Dispatch as any Man whatever." [29] Probably Rochester meant only that Wycherley was careful to perfect his work, in contrast to the slipshod Shadwell, who said that a correct play would take a year to write but who rather prided himself on not taking sufficient pains. Wycherley, as a gentleman writer, had no need to hasten; and, as an artist, he would not leave his work unfinished.

Rochester went on to sneer that Dryden tried to achieve the elegant erotic manner of the court wits—"For he to be a tearing *Blade,* thought fit"—but only succeeded in being coarse. In closing, Rochester expressed his scorn for the rabble's judgment: it is enough for him if Sedley, Shadwell, Sheppard, Wycherley, Godolphin, Butler, Dorset, and Buckingham approve his works.[30] This group mingles noblemen and writers, but the writers were carefully selected. Perhaps Rochester wrote this poem to amuse a party of friends who were visiting him in the country during one of his periodic exiles from court, and his final list of names —a haphazard selection from among the court wits—may represent the men present at the time.[31]

In "A Session of the Poets" (1676 or 1677) Rochester even more clearly distinguished Wycherley from other playwrights. The poem represents Apollo deciding which of them should be laureate. Dryden, the first contender, is contemptuously dismissed because it is thought he is joining the clergy. Then comes Etherege, who may not "be pardon'd" for failing to write a play in seven years. Then "Brawny *Wicherley*" comes forward, who is rejected only because he is "too good for the Place": "No *Gentle-*

man Writer, that office shou'd bear," but only "a *Trader* in *Wit.*"
Shadwell, who appears next, lacks sufficient wit for the position,
and so on with the other prominent playwrights of the day.[32]
What is significant is that Wycherley alone qualified as a gentleman, though Etherege was one of the court wits; moreover,
Rochester, censorious as he was, could find nothing to say against
him, as he did against all the others. Evidently Wycherley com-
manded respect, even from this flippant rake.

Only two of Wycherley's letters from this period are extant.
In the summer of 1671, he exchanged coarsely familiar verse-
letters with Shadwell, who was visiting in the country. Replying
to Shadwell's request for news, Wycherley told him about the
prorogation of Parliament and about the reopening of the playhouses after the official period of mourning for the duchess of
York's death:

> The Players, who had lost their Tongues
> For Grief, again now stretch their Lungs,
> And drunken Punk and Fop do sit
> And brawl and sweat and stink in Pit;
> And then in *Hide-Park* do repair
> To make a Dust and take no Air.[33]

Wycherley's other letter, dated August 20, 1677, sends the London news to the earl of Mulgrave, who was on military duty in
France. He writes as an equal of Mulgrave himself and of Mulgrave's friend Lord Middleton, who is so lazy that "if the whole
Army were routed, he would be kill'd, not to be at the Trouble
of running away." Wycherley has little news to report since the
Town is "empty." Dryden is in Northamptonshire; Wycherley
has lately drunk Mulgrave's health with the duke of Buckingham; the critic Thomas Rymer has just torn in pieces Mulgrave's
favorite Beaumont and Fletcher plays, and the wits have decided who is to answer him.[34] At about this time, Wycherley had
his portrait painted by Peter Lely, the most fashionable painter
of the day. The picture shows a handsome, fleshy face, framed
in the luxuriant curls of the period. The sitter is virile, modish,
and intensely self-assured.[35]

Once Wycherley tried to use his friendship with Buckingham
for the benefit of Samuel Butler, who had associated with the
court wits in the early 1670's, but was later in great need.

Wycherley "had made it his Business for some Time, to engage the Duke to an interview over a Bottle, where Mr. *Butler* might have the Opportunity of exerting his good Qualities and pleasant Humour." Finally, Wycherley managed to arrange a meeting of the three of them at a tavern, and all seemed to be going well, until "of a suddain they heard the squeaking of Fiddles, and the chattering of Whores in an adjacent Room; this was a Temptation the Duke cou'd not resist, he gives them the slip, and cou'd never be afterwards fix'd" to renew the opportunity.[36] The witty aristocrats forgot about Butler, who died destitute in 1680.

Wycherley's good nature, evident in this episode, was conspicuous throughout his life. At this period, it is indicated mainly by negative evidence: Wycherley, alone among the court wits, seems never to have been engaged in discreditable episodes. He was never involved in a duel, never in trouble with the law, never attacked in a libel. The few personal attacks that survive among his poems are mild and gentle compared to those of his contemporaries, and he seldom mentions names. It was an intensely contentious age—Dryden was constantly engaged in vituperative quarrels—but there is no record of Wycherley's being involved in any.

His clear record becomes significant when one contrasts him with his associates. Rochester and Etherege, after disturbing the town of Epsom one night and beating several unoffending citizens, ran off and left a friend to die in the ensuing scuffle. Rochester devoted his genius to writing obscene lampoons on his erstwhile friends at court and, with some justification, was characterized in *An Essay on Satyr* as "Mean in each action, lewd in every limb, / Manners themselves are mischievous in him." [37] Dorset and Sedley scandalized the public with drunken blasphemy and indecent exposure. Buckingham took Lady Shrewsbury to his home after killing her husband in a notorious duel; and, when his devoted wife protested against living in the same house with that woman, he consoled her with the news that he had provided a coach to send her home to her father.[38]

III *The Gentleman Dancing-Master*

Meanwhile, Wycherley's second play, *The Gentleman Dancing-Master,* was produced by the Duke's Company in Dorset Garden on February 6, 1672,[39] the Theatre Royal in Bridges Street having burned down the preceding January. Possibly because of the change in company, more probably because of the insipidity of the plot, the piece was not very successful: "It lasted but six days, being like't but indifferently." [40] *The Gentleman Dancing-Master* is certainly thin in comparison to *Love in a Wood* or to the great Restoration comedies. Attempting to correct the disunity which was the main flaw of *Love in a Wood*, Wycherley focused on a single situation, one which was not sufficiently substantial to carry a whole play, and developed it at tedious length.

A young girl, Hippolita, has been kept completely secluded from men and is about to be married by her tyrannical father, James Formal, to her foolish cousin, Mr. Parris. These two extremists have been so taken with foreign manners that they insist on being called Don Diego Formal and Monsieur de Paris. Through cleverly manipulating her cousin Parris, Hippolita finds out the name of an eligible young man, Gerrard; gets him to come to her room; and, when her father discovers him, passes him off as a dancing master. Since Gerrard is mystified by the situation and cannot even dance, many farcical complications ensue. At one point, when the young lovers have the opportunity to elope, Hippolita herself holds back in order to be sure that Gerrard truly loves her. But, in the end, he demonstrates his love for Hippolita; and the lovers outwit her foolish father and suitor by exploiting their conceit.

Anne Righter argues that Hippolita and Gerrard are kept apart by genuine psychological obstacles, not merely by contrived external ones, and that the play shows how "two intelligent people have succeeded in establishing an equilibrium of realism and romanticism in their relationship." [41] Gratifying as it would be to find more substance in *The Gentleman Dancing-Master*, the argument seems more ingenious than convincing. Actually, the basis of the lovers' relationship is purely romantic, and the main reason for Hippolita's delay is to extend the basic comic situation and to complicate the general confusion by causing Gerrard to wonder whether he is the dupe instead of Monsieur.

The comic situation and the "humours" of the two principal fools in the play—the dogmatic hispanicized father and the foppish frenchified suitor—are required to carry more humorous

weight than they can bear. Some scenes, however, must have
been hilarious on stage. For example, the last part of Act IV
brings all the major characters on stage and reveals each one
placed in an amusingly false position by the deceptions which
he is practicing or which are being practiced on him. Hippolita,
who may have just outsmarted herself by rebuffing Gerrard in
order to test his affection, must conciliate him and, at the same
time, maintain the pretense to her father and her aunt, Mrs.
Caution, that he is merely giving her a dancing lesson. Gerrard,
still not sufficiently exasperated to betray Hippolita, continues to
blunder along as a dancing master, while surreptitiously giving
vent to his anger. Mrs. Caution, realizing the truth, keeps trying
to expose Gerrard; but her brother and nephew, the two who
should be most concerned to prevent an elopement, refuse to
listen to her. Don Diego will not admit that anyone could have
more penetration than he does, and Monsieur de Paris is too
assured of his own sophistication and attractiveness to suspect
that his fiancée might be interested in another man. Monsieur
knows more of the situation than the older generation but believes that he and Hippolita are making a fool of Gerrard as
well as the others. Though he is in fact the most egregious dupe,
his conceit and his partial knowledge keep him laughing at everybody else.

The dialogue which ensues, while not particularly witty, skillfully exploits the humor of double meanings and cross-purposes:

Monsieur: Well, how goes the Dancing forward? what my Aunt here
to disturb 'em again?
Don Diego: Come, come. [Gerrard leads (Hippolita) about.
Caution: I say stand off, thou shalt not come near, avoid, Satan, as
they say.
Don Diego: Nay then we shall have it, Nephew, hold her a little,
that she may not disturb 'em, come, now away with her.
Gerrard: One, two, and a Coupee. Fool'd and abus'd. [Aside
Caution: Wilt thou lay violent hands upon thy own natural Aunt,
Wretch? [The Monsieur holding Caution.
Don Diego: Come, about with her.
Gerrard: One, two, three, four, and turn round. By such a piece of
Innocency. [Aside
Caution: Dost thou see, Fool, how he squeezes her hand?
Monsieur: That won't do, Aunt.

Hippolita: Pray, Master, have patience, and let's mind our business.
Don Diego: Why did you anger him then, Hussy, look you?
Caution: Do you see how she smiles in his face, and squeezes his hand now?
Monsieur: Your Servant, Aunt, that won't do, I say.
Hippolita: Have patience, Master.
Gerrard: I am become her sport, *[aside]* one, two, three, Death, Hell, and the Devil.
Don Diego: Ay, they are three indeed; but pray have patience.
Caution: Do you see how she leers upon him and clings to him, can you suffer it?
Monsieur: Ay, ay.
Gerrard: One, two, and a slur; can you be so unconcern'd after all?
Don Diego: What, is she unconcern'd! Hussy, mind your bus'ness.
Gerrard: One, two, three, and turn round, one, two, fall back, Hell and Damnation.
Don Diego: Ay, people, fall back indeed into Hell and Damnation, Heav'n knows.
Gerrard: One, two, three, and your Honour: I can fool no longer.
Caution: Nor will I be withel'd any longer like a poor Hen in her Pen, while the Kite is carrying away her Chicken before her face.

The conversation proceeds to draw out the fools' self-delusion and the wits' ingenuity, up to Monsieur's exit line: "Lord! that people shou'd be made such Fools of, hah, hah." [42]
    Wycherley took the central situation of his play from Calderón's *El Maestro de Danzar*, in which the heroine, entertaining her suitor in her father's house, passes him off as a dancing master when her father appears. As in his previous adaptation from Calderón, Wycherley aimed primarily at wit and comic bustle, instead of the romantic atmosphere of the original. He invented the characters of Monsieur de Paris, Mrs. Caution, and two prostitutes who exploit Monsieur through his vanity; and he turned Don Diego from an ordinary heavy father into a ridiculous Hispanomaniac. Monsieur's inept Francophile affectations—his devotion to extreme French styles of dress, his constant use of mispronounced French words, his confusion of insult with gay raillery, his contempt for his own country and inordinate pride in his "Eyrè *Francèz*"—were characteristic of fops in plays and in real life. The type was first dramatized in James Howard's *The English Mounsieur* (produced in 1666), to which Hippolita

alludes in the play.[43] All the fools, as is usual in Restoration comedy, mistake externals for reality: Don Diego mistakes pomposity and suspicion for wisdom; Monsieur de Paris, inane briskness, for wit; Mrs. Caution, technical chastity preserved by force, for virtue.

The device by which the imprisoned Hippolita manages to get a message to Gerrard through his rival, Monsieur, was adapted from Molière's *School for Husbands,* where Isabella communicates with Valère through Sganarelle, the oppressive guardian who intends to marry her. Though both girls fear they may be criticized for boldness,[44] the young lady of Restoration London shows more initiative and independence. Isabella merely responds to Valère's demonstration of love; but Hippolita, having no man to turn to, has to make the first overtures to Gerrard.

The most appealing feature of *The Gentleman Dancing-Master* is the character of Hippolita and the enlightened view of marriage she represents. She is witty and resourceful, like the typical Restoration heroine, with the brave self-reliance and unsentimental honesty which come from an independent spirit. After talking a little with Gerrard, she says to herself:

Ih—h—like this man strangely, I was going to say lov'd him. Courage then, *Hippolita,* make use of the only opportunity thou canst have to enfranchize thy self: Women formerly (they say) never knew how to make use of their time till it was past; but let it not be said so of a young Woman of this Age; my damn'd Aunt will be stirring presently: well then, courage, I say, *Hippolita,* thou art full fourteen years old, shift for thy self.

She claims her right to "all the innocent liberty of the Town" and has no scruples about flouting her father's tyrannical authority. Yet she wants to use her freedom for wholesome, moral ends; Wycherley emphasizes the point that she is virtuous. She wants to make a satisfying marriage, but she is not lascivious like her hypocritically precise aunt or her earthy maid, Prue, who longs only for a sexual outlet. Nor is she unpleasantly knowing; she is horrified at the idea of marrying a fool, while Prue, judging by the usual standards of Restoration society, thinks a fool would do as well for a husband as any other man.[45]

Perhaps "those Ladies, who are never precise but at a Play" will censure Hippolita's forwardness in getting herself a husband, "but sure though I give my self and fortune away franckly, without the consent of my Friends, my confidence is less than theirs, who stand off only for separate maintenance." A woman who gives herself for love is more truly modest than one who waits demurely while her family sells her for the most advantageous financial arrangement. Wycherley exposes what the conventional mercenary marriage really was: a woman who accepts a fop because her parents threaten to withhold her inheritance if she does not obey them "Is but a lawful Wench for gain." [46]

The fools in the play share a low conception of marriage. Don Diego thinks it is perfectly suitable for a woman to hate her husband; "that's the reason we wise *Spaniards* . . . will be sure our Wives shall fear us." Monsieur de Paris sees "little difference betwixt keeping a Wench and Marriage," except that "Marriage is a little the cheaper," while "the other is the more honourable."[47] Don Diego, the rigid tyrant over women, and Monsieur, the nonchalant coxcomb who does not care about them, anticipate Pinchwife and Sparkish, respectively, in *The Country-Wife*. They are not nearly so effective, however, because Wycherley conceived them primarily as national caricatures. They are composed of superficial—and dated—mannerisms and are not much more psychologically profound than the clothes to which they attach so much importance. Wycherley had not yet thought through the psychological forces underlying social affectations; therefore, his characters do not have significance as embodiments of human nature. Hippolita is the only substantial character in the play.

When Wycherley published *The Gentleman Dancing-Master* at the end of the year, he gave it a Horatian epigraph: "It is not enough to make your hearer grin with laughter—though even in that there is some merit." He might have been claiming a seriousness for the play which in truth it lacked, for it is less a moral satire than an overextended farce. On the other hand, the epigraph may represent a wry self-judgment: perhaps Wycherley realized that *The Gentleman Dancing-Master* did not offer enough, that it wanted a serious theme. Moral purpose, suggested in *Love in a Wood* and virtually dropped in Wycherley's second play, was to become central in his mature work, shaping *The Country-Wife* and distorting *The Plain-Dealer*. It would have been in character for Wycherley to cover his mortification over the relative failure of his play by publishing it with a self-deprecatory epigraph.

The Epilogue to *The Gentleman Dancing-Master* is addressed to the citizens in the audience, since "all Gentlemen must pack to Sea."[48] War with the Dutch was impending—it was actually declared the following month—and the young gentlemen of the Town were volunteering for service. Buckingham, who was made colonel of a regiment, saw to it that Wycherley got a commission as captain-lieutenant, which meant a particularly close association with the colonel. Buckingham and his officers received their commissions on June 19, 1672.

There is no reason to suppose that Wycherley had any knowledge of soldiering or ever saw military action, for the Third Dutch War was a naval one as far as England was concerned. Many officers of the period were amateurs who were chosen by their colonels for congeniality. They seem to have spent most of their time visiting and gambling. Buckingham, probably accompanied by Wycherley, spent 1673 raising troops in Yorkshire and drilling them on Blackheath Common, just outside London. When the regiment was disbanded at the end of the war, Wycherley was made captain of Buckingham's company. His commission was signed on February 28, 1674; and he resigned it a week later.[49]

Perhaps it was when he joined the army that Wycherley moved permanently from the Inner Temple. Although he had never been a serious student of the law, there must have been some point when he definitely rejected a legal career and, accordingly, moved out of the Temple. A possibly autobiographical passage in his last play, *The Plain-Dealer*, might indicate when he did so. Freeman, a character who sometimes speaks for Wycherley, is a navy lieutenant who has been a student at an Inn of Court, but is "too good a Joker, to have any Law" in his head. He confesses he was once a lawyer, "but was fain to leave the Law, out of Conscience, and fall to making false Musters; rather chose to Cheat the King, than his Subjects; Plunder, rather than take Fees."[50] Since there seems to be no dramatic reason for Freeman to have a legal background, it seems likely that Wycherley put in these details from his own experience, transposing army to navy because Freeman had to be lieutenant to a sea captain. His army commission provided an alternative career to the law and might have been what decided Wycherley to make a long-desired break.

In any case, after serving in the army, Wycherley lived for many years at the Widow Hilton's in Bow Street near Covent Garden Square, opposite the Cock Tavern.[51] Bow Street was broad and lined "with very good Houses . . . resorted unto by Gentry for Lodgings."[52] The district was singularly convenient for a man of Wycherley's tastes: the Drury Lane Theatre, where his two major plays were produced, was near the Square, and the fashionable Rose Tavern adjoined it. Will's Coffee-House, frequented by the court wits and regularly attended by Dryden, was at the corner of Bow and Russell streets. It was usual for a prosperous bachelor in Wycherley's time to take two or three rooms in a well-appointed house and to dine with friends at a tavern. Dinner, the big meal of the day, served at twelve or one o'clock, could cost anything from a shilling at an ordinary to eight shillings and sixpence at Chatelin's. After dining one could go to the theater and then for a walk or a drive in Saint James's Park. Supper would often merge into a drinking party.

While Wycherley had produced *The Gentleman Dancing-Master* only a few months after *Love in a Wood*, he was less quick to turn out his next play: probably he was not only discouraged but resolved to be sure that he had enough and properly developed material. When *The Country-Wife* was produced in January, 1675, his poor success with *The Gentleman Dancing-Master* still rankled; for in his conciliatory prologue he spoke of himself as "The late so bafled Scribler."[53]

CHAPTER 3

The Country-Wife

I *The Role of Horner*

THE "bafled Scribler" completely restored his reputation with the triumphant success of his next play. *The Country-Wife* was produced on January 12, 1675 at the Theatre Royal in Drury Lane[1] and immediately passed into the repertory. It dramatizes Horner's scheme to gain access to the wives of suspicious husbands by pretending to have been made impotent by venereal disease. Believing Horner innocuous, Sir Jaspar Fidget encourages his wife to consort with him; and Horner is soon having affairs with Lady Fidget and two of her friends. Pinchwife, who has reluctantly come to London with his new wife—Margery, the country-wife of the title—in order to marry his sister, Alithea, to Sparkish, has not heard that Horner is supposed to be impotent and frantically tries to keep Margery away from him. Not only do his efforts fail, but he involuntarily cooperates in bringing Margery and Horner together. Meanwhile Horner's friend Harcourt has fallen in love with Alithea; and, when she becomes convinced that she is not morally obligated to marry Sparkish, Harcourt persuades her to marry him instead. In the end, the cuckolded husbands are pacified by being assured by everyone, including the ladies who know the contrary, that Horner is physically incapable of injuring their honor.

The Country-Wife is a masterpiece first of all because it is hilariously funny. Wycherley used to particularly good effect his comic device of speeches which a dupe interprets one way, but which the intelligent characters and the audience understand to have a different meaning. When the would-be wit Sparkish overhears the true wits plotting to bubble (cheat) a fool of his mistress, he is too conceited to realize they are referring to himself; and he unhesitatingly chimes in: "Who is that, that is to be bubled? Faith let me snack [share], I han't met with a buble since Christmas." [2]

The funniest *double-entendre* conversation in the play occurs in Horner's lodgings, where Lady Fidget has come to lie with him. When her husband unexpectedly appears, she claims to have come for some of Horner's china, of which he has a particularly fine collection. After she has got what she came for, her like-minded friend Mrs. (that is, Miss) Squeamish appears and clamors for some too; she is pursued by her grandmother, who is vainly trying to keep her chaste. In the conversation which follows, the older generation, Sir Jaspar Fidget and Old Lady Squeamish, blithely interpret *china* to mean *china;* but the young people understand that it is something else:

Lady Fidget: And I have been toyling and moyling, for the pretti'st piece of China, my Dear [husband].
Horner: Nay, she has been too hard for me do what I cou'd.
Squeamish: Oh, Lord, I'le have some China too, good Mr. *Horner,* don't think to give other people China, and me none, come in with me too.
Horner: Upon my honour I have none left now.
Squeamish: Nay, nay, I have known you deny your China before now, but you shan't put me off so, come—
Horner: This Lady had the last there.
Lady Fidget: Yes indeed Madam, to my certain knowledge he has no more left.
Squeamish: O but it may be he may have some you could not find.
Lady Fidget: What d'y think if he had had any left, I would not have had it too, for we women of quality never think we have China enough.
Horner: Do not take it ill, I cannot make China for you all, but I will have a Rol-waggon [a cylindrical vase, phallic in shape] for you too, another time.
Squeamish: Thank you dear Toad. *[To Horner aside.*
Lady Fidget [who has been given the impression she is the only person informed of Horner's secret]: What do you mean by that promise?
Horner: Alas, she has an innocent, literal understanding. *[Apart to Lady Fidget*
[Old] Lady Squeamish: Poor Mr. *Horner,* he has enough to doe to please you all, I see. . . . Poor Gentleman I pitty you.[3]

The double meanings are sustained throughout, and each group plausibly interprets what is said in terms of its own knowledge. As the conversation is drawn out—just to the right extent—it becomes funnier and funnier, as one wonders how long the two meanings can be sustained, and the latent meaning becomes increasingly obscene.

The most richly humorous character in the play is the country-wife, Margery Pinchwife, whose sexual union with Horner is the aim of the main plot. As a natural character thrust into a highly artificial society, she is both endearing and ludicrous. Happily unaware of the social restraints of prudence and propriety, she proclaims with equal openness her enjoyment of oranges and of Horner's kisses—why shouldn't she enjoy the kisses of a handsome man, so long as his breath is sweet?

The Country-Wife is not, however, a mere farce, written only to amuse by double meaning and incongruity: its humor illustrates character and theme. Sparkish keeps misinterpreting speeches which are perfectly evident to everybody else because he is too self-absorbed to be aware of anyone's feelings but his own. When the ladies squabble over Horner's china, really meaning Horner himself, there is a symbolic suggestion that Horner's compulsive lechery has reduced him to an object instead of a free agent. In addition, since china is really refined and decorated earth, it is an appropriate symbol for the sexuality of people like Lady Fidget, which is earthiness disguised almost beyond recognition.[4] Margery's simple-mindedness does more than arouse laughter by its incongruity; for, at the same time that the sophisticated characters show up her ridiculous uncouthness, she brings out their ridiculous or contemptible artificiality. As Wycherley recognized in his epigraph to *The Gentleman Dancing-Master*, it is not enough to make the reader laugh; a great comedy must say something.

Moreover, Wycherley had found a significant theme for *The Country-Wife*, to give it substance, to unify it and at the same time afford rich variety. His theme is the selfishness which pervaded sexual relationships in his society. Casting a penetrating eye on the social scene, Wycherley saw that the most brilliant gentlemen of the Town pursued women not as wives, not even as mistresses, but as wenches—moving from one sexual partner to another, with nothing to hold them once the sexual itch was gratified. He saw that the ladies, equally exploitative, were out to satisfy their lust or greed without any thought of love. He saw that the contemporary marriage of convenience encouraged husbands to act like jailers and wives to abandon chastity and fidelity, although they were still sufficiently influenced by the traditional code to conceal their sexuality with hypocrisy.

In *The Country-Wife* Wycherley exposed what was wrong in his contemporaries' attitudes toward love and marriage, and he suggested a more decent basis for relationships between the sexes.[5] He did this through three intertwined plots, which present three self-absorbed men—Sparkish, Pinchwife, and Sir Jaspar Fidget—who lose their women; in contrast to them, Harcourt, the one man who genuinely loves, wins a good wife. Wycherley pointed and unified his satire through the character of Horner, a witty rake who is a spectacularly successful member of his society. Through his wit, Horner exposes the rationalizations of his fellow characters. Through his pretense that he is a eunuch, he draws out the meanness of the foolish men in the play and the lust of the lady pretenders to virtue. He exposes the hollowness of "honor" in a society where "a Man can't come amongst virtuous Women . . . but upon the same terms, as Men are admitted into the great Turks Seraglio." [6] The overwhelming importance of Horner's sexual condition in the world of the play suggests the overemphasis on sex in the Restoration world.

Some interpreters, such as John H. Wilson, interpret Horner as Wycherley's unqualified ideal: as a libertine who gratifies his natural impulses without inner scruples or outward restraints, he is equally free of hypocrisy and of reverence for forms like marriage. Others find him horrifying or contemptible. Bonamy Dobrée sees him as a "grim, nightmare" personification of lechery; Rose Zimbardo, as a parasite-satirist, more intelligent but just as debased, and just as much an object of satire, as the knaves and dupes on whom he preys. Marvin Mudrick makes an illuminating comparison between Horner, whose feigned impotence brings out the lust of his society, and Volpone, whose feigned illness brings out the greed of his. Anne Righter points out that, like Volpone, Horner "is a monomaniac who pays too great a price for his undeniable success." [7]

Probably Wycherley meant Horner to be a true wit, who is admirable because he clearly understands himself and others, though at the same time he plainly suggested comically sordid aspects to the character. Horner's attitude toward sexual relationships is squalid. He maintains that keeping is better than marriage because women, like soldiers, are "made constant and loyal by good pay, rather than by Oaths and Covenants." [8] In two days he beds four women, for none of whom he feels anything beyond lust. While such behavior was not shocking to a Restoration man-about-town, it was not ideal either: the typical Restoration hero is capable of falling in love and marrying, and in this very play Harcourt and Alithea demonstrate a better sexual relationship than Horner's affairs with women he despises. Moreover, on the occasion when he is forced by his amatory entanglements to belie Alithea in order to protect Margery, he tells what his contemporaries would condemn as a shameful lie. Wycherley did not, of course, criticize Horner severely: the spectator is supposed to admire Horner's dexterity and should not be horrified by his libertinism in a play in which all sexual sins are venial.

Horner's pose as a eunuch, besides emphasizing the exclusively physical nature of his interest in women, symbolically suggests that—for all his virility—he is something less than a man. Although physically complete, he misses part of love just as surely as a eunuch does. His declaration that he can't be a husband is not entirely camouflage; he is incapable of the emotions and idealism necessary in marital love.[9] Ironically, this aggressive male gets himself into the comic position of being exploited by women, as he must spend his time shopping for china and letting them cheat him at cards. Finally, in the scene where the ladies compete for his china, he becomes a passive victim, fought over by rapacious females. This possessor of a seraglio finds himself, like King Charles II, dominated by his wenches.

Horner's most important function in the play, however, is masterful manipulation of his fellow characters to amuse himself, to reveal their real natures, and to control them through their pretensions and weaknesses. Most obviously, he exposes Lady Fidget—a loveless, greedy nymphomaniac who makes constant professions of honor and virtue—and her like-minded friends. They are delighted to sleep with a man who, supposedly a eunuch, cannot injure their reputations; and their guardians are equally delighted to see them in the company of one with whom (it is thought) they cannot possibly commit adultery. Technical chastity is all that Sir Jaspar Fidget and Old Lady Squeamish mean by woman's virtue; they, like Mrs. Caution in *The Gentleman Dancing-Master,* believe that a girl cannot possibly be wicked if she has not seen a man.[10]

Perhaps Wycherley was too heavy-handed in his exposure of these women: in the climactic drinking scene in Horner's lodgings, they confess more than is realistic; and the naked ugliness of the resulting picture is inconsistent with the gay tone of the play as a whole. It is too fantastic for a woman like Lady Fidget to admit openly, even in drink, that her public modesty is an unmistakable sign of her private lust. Wycherley's other pretenders in the play expose themselves unwittingly through transparent rationalizations. Evidently Wycherley was so revolted by Lady Fidget's type that he could not control his disgust when writing about her. Possibly his experience with the duchess of Cleveland contributed to his loathing for voraciously lustful ladies of condition.

Earlier in the play, Wycherley handled Lady Fidget with more tact. In the middle of a discussion with her friends on whether it is less guilty to take upper or lower-class lovers, she turns on one who mentions pleasure: "Fye, fye, fye, for shame Sister, whither shall we ramble? be continent in your discourse, or I shall hate you." Trying to find out whether Horner might reveal his virility and thus betray her if they were to have an affair, she is at last forced to abandon her usual refined circumlocution: "I mean, if you'l give me leave to speak obscenely, you might tell." For Lady Fidget, the only obscenity is the nakedness of truth.

The best example of Lady Fidget's hypocrisy, one which has gone so far that it seems now to delude even herself, occurs when she arrives to lie with Horner. Wycherley prepares for the climactic encounter by stressing the word "honor" nine times in successive speeches by the Quack, Horner, and Lady Fidget herself; this excessive use, or abuse, of the word undermines its meaning to suggest that "honor" had become an empty term in fashionable Restoration society. Hesitating at the door of Horner's bedroom, Lady Fidget stipulates again that he must have a care of her dear honor. Horner retorts that any more talk of her honor will make him "incapable to wrong it; to talk of Honour in the mysteries of Love, is like talking of Heaven . . . in an operation of Witchcraft, just when you are employing the Devil [this has an obscene double meaning, more appropriate to love than witchcraft], it makes the charm impotent." Lady Fidget rebukes him: "Nay, fie, let us not be smooty" (smutty).[11] Here Wycherley makes her expose her hypocrisy in a plausible way, without dropping the mask which such a woman always wears. Furthermore, the indirectness keeps the dialogue comic rather than disgusting.

II *Sparkish versus Pinchwife*

Lady Fidget and her friends, who affect the very virtue they most lack, represent a stock Restoration butt. All true wits of the period would agree with Horner's condemnation of "all that force Nature, and wou'd be still what she forbids 'em; Affectation is her greatest Monster." [12] Would-be wits, like Sparkish, were satirized for the same reason. But Wycherley deepened the significance of this stock character by using him to illuminate the theme: he made Sparkish a mouthpiece for the modish attitude toward marriage, which is shown to be ridiculous by the exaggerations and misinterpretations of a would-be wit.

Since the true wits to whom he attaches himself sneer at marriage, Sparkish does too. "The best, and truest love in the World" cannot be matrimonial love, he tells Alithea. This opinion was common among the wits, though they would not have been stupid enough to express it to their brides; it is characteristic of the would-be wit to give vent to what he thinks is a smart saying regardless of its inappropriateness. Sparkish worries that marriage will spoil his wit, even though he intends to continue seeing his witty friends and making similes. Unlike the true wit, Harcourt, who can change his opinions under the influence of love—"till now I never thought I shou'd have envy'd . . . any Man about to marry, but you [Sparkish] have the best excuse for Marriage I ever knew" [13]—Sparkish will always remain the same, parroting the opinions of "us wits."

Sparkish eschews jealousy because he considers it a bourgeois attitude. Since he stupidly thinks that the way to be a wit is to act differently from a citizen in all respects, he sneers at the legitimate restraints of an engagement. Since he mistakes the sophisticated wit's emotional control for lack of emotion, he thinks it ill bred to take anything seriously, including his marriage. He pretends to be equally unaffected by love, jealousy, or anger: "we wits rail and make love often, but to shew our parts; as we have no affections, so we have no malice." [14] Like all of Wycherley's false wits, he confuses wit with heartlessness and, in spite of his claim, with malice. It is only he and the equally foolish Sir Jaspar who gloat over Horner's supposed misfortune; the true wits do their best to console him; they only bait people such as Pinchwife who deserve punishment.[15]

So free from jealousy is Sparkish that he claims he would like to have rivals in a wife, so she would seem like a kept mistress, a more fashionable possession. "Though my hunger is now my sawce," he tells Horner, "and I can fall on heartily without [added stimulation] . . . the time will come, when a Rival will be as good sawce for a married man to a wife, as an Orange to Veale." Horner takes this up wittily, at the same time showing his disgust at Sparkish's selfish unconcern: "O thou damn'd Rogue, thou hast set my teeth on edge with thy [sour] Orange." Sparkish completely misses the moral criticism because he is so intent on carrying on the simile, which he lamely does: "Then let's to dinner, there I was with you againe, come." [16] The similes in this play are seldom merely decorative: they reveal character. Throughout, characters who do not rightly understand love compare women to food.[17]

Sparkish can be so unconcerned because he is utterly self-centered. Wycherley shows how the characteristic narcissism of the fop distorts a man's attitude toward women. Sparkish is so absorbed in himself that he is practically unaware of other people. That is why he allows Harcourt to court Alithea before his face: all he can think of is his own image of himself as a person so sophisticated that he is immune to jealousy. Since Harcourt only exists for him as an appendage to himself, he cannot conceive of his having separate interests; Harcourt's wish to break off the match must therefore result from his regret at losing Sparkish's company. He has brought Harcourt to see Alithea out of a combination of vanity and malice, because he likes to show her off and to gloat over less fortunate people, just as he likes "to shew fine Clothes, at a Play-house the first day, and count money before poor Rogues." [18] Since Sparkish already thinks of Alithea as his property (like his clothes), it does not occur to him that she might decide to leave him. Although these courtship scenes are farcically exaggerated, they are acceptable in context because they are true to character: an extremely selfish person can be practically oblivious to other people's feelings.[19]

Confronted with evidence that Alithea has been unfaithful, Sparkish's reaction is, "But who would have thought a woman could have been false to me." He is angry not because he is losing her but because she appears to have perversely deceived "a Gentleman of wit and pleasure about the Town." He does not hesitate to believe in her guilt because he has not paid enough attention to her to learn that she is honorable and because he cannot conceal for a moment a wound to his precious self-esteem. As with Pinchwife, jealousy is a purely selfish emotion, resulting from injured self-esteem and lack of faith in other people—not, as the Restoration still liked to think, a sign of love. The true wit Harcourt, in contrast, is both more concerned about Alithea's loyalty and more firm in his belief in her because he truly cares about her. True wits, in Wycherley, are always capable of genuine feeling for other people. Even the hardened rake Horner feels sorry that Alithea is to be thrown away upon Sparkish and Harcourt to be frustrated in his love.[20]

Pinchwife illustrates the traditional "respectable" view of marriage, which is as selfish and more harmful than the fashionable libertinism travestied by Sparkish. Wycherley has Horner expose Pinchwife by foiling his would-be wise schemes to keep his wife faithful and by making quiet comments which show the absurdity of his "honor" and the odious selfishness of his attitude toward women. Pinchwife, a superannuated rake of forty-nine, has just married. Marriage, for him, is purely a sexual and financial arrangement; he says of his sister's impending wedding: "I must give *Sparkish* to morrow five thousand pound to lye with my Sister." For himself, because—as Pinchwife constantly boasts—he knows the Town, he has chosen Margery, a country girl so simple that she cannot be unfaithful to him. Nevertheless, he keeps her locked up and, when forced to take her out, insists that she be disguised. Alithea suggests that Margery simply put

on her mask, which would attract no attention; but the wise
Pinchwife makes her dress in boy's clothes and pretend to be
her own brother.[21] The result is that Horner can kiss her freely,
while Pinchwife stands helplessly by, unable to reveal that she
is in fact a woman on whom he alone has a proprietary claim.

Pinchwife shows, in exaggerated form, the usual Restoration
cynicism about woman's virtue. He is a would-be wit because
the worldly wisdom on which he prides himself is actually only
mechanical suspiciousness, and it enables him to outwit no one
but himself. His horror of being "a Cuckold, like a credulous
Cit," parallels Sparkish's of being "jealous, like a Country
Bumpkin." [22]

Mainly, however, Pinchwife's contempt for women results from
the view of marriage traditional in his patriarchal society and
cherished by the self-righteous citizens who were shocked by
libertine wits: that marriage is a divinely ordained compact to
give a man exclusive rights over a woman. According to this
view, a wife is not a person but a piece of property; and her
husband's main concern about her is to keep other men out
of his "own Free-hold." She should be kept ignorant so as not
to give trouble to her lord and ruler. Nature and heaven intended
women to be "plain, open, silly, and fit for slaves." Pinchwife's
attitude was by no means unthinkable in his day, when even
a man so high-minded as John Milton made his ideal woman say
to her husband: "God is thy Law, thou mine: to know no more /
Is woman's happiest knowledge and her praise." [23]

But Wycherley acutely saw the poisonous self-centeredness of
this view and the misery to which it leads. Men like Pinchwife,
who expect unquestioning devotion from women without offering
anything in return, are bound to be disappointed. Their unloving,
exploitative attitude leads them to project their own hostility
onto women. Thus Pinchwife defends his behavior: "if we do
not cheat women, they'll cheat us; and fraud may be justly
used with secret enemies, of which a Wife is the most dangerous."
Unable to appreciate any high qualities in women, such men
necessarily find them more trouble than they are worth: "Wife
and Sister are names which make us expect Love and duty,
pleasure and comfort, but we find 'em plagues and torments, and
are equally, though differently troublesome to their keeper; for

we have as much a-doe to get people to lye with our Sisters, as
to keep 'em from lying with our Wives." [24] Wycherley saw the
sadism in this traditional attitude: Pinchwife's name is significant, and it would be quite in character for him to kill Margery's pet
squirrel, as she fears.

Although Pinchwife's own declarations of his views are sufficiently exaggerated to show their folly and selfishness, Horner
often draws him out. Observing Pinchwife's low conception of
marriage, Horner asks him why he does not just keep a mistress
instead. Pinchwife answers that he "cou'd never keep a Whore
to my self," and Horner's sardonic comment, "So then you only
marry'd to keep a Whore to your self," is an accurate statement
of Pinchwife's aspirations. When Pinchwife blusters about his
"honor" to keep Horner away from Margery, he gives Horner
the opportunity to puncture his claim to a quality which he really
knows nothing about. To Pinchwife's threat that "my honour will
suffer no jesting . . . I will not be a Cuckold I say, there will be
danger in making me a Cuckold," Horner retorts, "Why, wert
thou not well cur'd of thy last clap?" [25] Pinchwife's "honor" is
just as negligible as Horner implies: it is nothing but his capacity
to prevent Margery by force from cuckolding him.

Although Pinchwife and Sparkish appear to be absolute op-
posites, they share the same low and selfish view of women.
Pinchwife's possessiveness and Sparkish's conceit have the same
effect. Each thinks of women only in terms of his own convenience: Margery exists to satisfy Pinchwife's sexual needs;
Alithea, to gratify Sparkish's vanity. Neither has any interest in
what the women themselves may feel, so long as Margery does
not disparage Pinchwife's honor nor Alithea Sparkish's parts.
Wycherley makes clear their underlying contempt for women:
Pinchwife wants his wife silly, and Sparkish remarks that "virtue
makes a Woman as troublesome, as a little reading, or learning."
Horner, on the other hand, a true wit despite his cynicism about
love, thinks that "wit is more necessary than beauty, and I think
no young Woman ugly that has it, and no handsome Woman
agreeable without it." [26]

Wycherley underlines the parallel between them by letting
each criticize the other's fault. Pinchwife is horrified by the fatuous complacency of Sparkish watching Harcourt woo his fiancée,

and Sparkish is right for once when he says: "we men of wit have amongst us a saying, that . . . you may keep your Wife as much as you will out of danger of infection, but if her constitution incline her" to cuckolding, "she'l have it sooner or later by the world." The parallel is reinforced by the parallel situations in which Wycherley places them. Sparkish watches Harcourt court Alithea because he is too complacent to realize what is going on; Pinchwife watches Horner court Margery in boy's disguise because, as a result of his own inept scheming, he cannot protest effectively without giving his plot away. He realizes that, with all his knowledge of the Town, he is in the same position as Sparkish: "was I not accusing another just now, for this rascally patience, in permitting his Wife to be kiss'd before his face?" [27]

Although the equally unsatisfactory husband Sir Jaspar Fidget seems to be different from Pinchwife and Sparkish, Wycherley shows that he too is selfish and contemptuous of women. His business is developing projects and Sparkish's is shining in society, but they are alike in running off to Whitehall and ignoring the legitimate claims of their women. Sir Jaspar's only concern about his wife, like Pinchwife's, is to prevent her from cuckolding him. Since he is civil, he seeks to do so by keeping her harmlessly occupied rather than by locking her up; but neither man cares for his wife as a person, so long as she can somehow be kept, with a minimum of effort on his part, from disgracing him. Although Sir Jaspar states his opinion more gently than Pinchwife, he too thinks of woman as an inferior animal. When he babbles of "that sweet, soft, gentle, tame, noble Creature Woman," Horner elicits what underlies his attitude by carrying on the thought: "So is that soft, gentle, tame, and more noble Creature a Spaniel." [28]

Sir Jaspar is just as eager to exploit Horner, by making him a sort of keeper for his wife, as Horner is to exploit him; their intentions are equally selfish. Despite all its cuckolding, the play is poetically just; for all three men who lose their women (temporarily or permanently) deserve to lose them. As P. F. Vernon points out, "Sir Jaspar actually forces Horner on to his wife, so that he can get away to his business; just as Sparkish forces Harcourt on Alithea, so that he can run off to the playhouse . . .

every effort [Pinchwife] makes to keep his wife in ignorance only helps to teach her what he wishes to conceal." It is symbolically appropriate when Pinchwife actually, physically leads his wife to Horner.[29] Wycherley shows that nothing but love can beget love; the selfish person who expects love for nothing is bound to be frustrated. Horner at least gives the ladies sexual pleasure.

III *The Right Way*

Alithea, the only virtuous woman in the play, deserves—and gets—more. She is very much a lady of her society—insisting on her right to "take the innocent liberty of the Town," but acquiescing in the conventionally acceptable marriage which her brother, Pinchwife, has arranged for her. (This marriage, to a man of her own class chosen by her brother, satisfied the ordinary Restoration standards. It was usual to marry without love, hoping that it would develop after marriage; if it did not, the couple would just jog along under the yoke as best they could.) Alithea rejects Harcourt's advances in order to preserve her reputation, since the match has gone too far to be broken off, and to avoid injustice to Sparkish: if he "be true, and what I think him to me, I must be so to him." [30] She values Sparkish because she generously interprets his lack of jealousy as proof that he appreciates her virtue.

Her conversation with Lucy, her maid, on the morning of her wedding probes her motives more deeply, finally exposing a slight taint of the selfishness which corrupted sexual relationships at the time. Lucy makes the valid point (not so obvious in the seventeenth century as now) that to marry a man without loving him is a greater wrong than to break an engagement. She says it is folly to expect love to develop afterward (by now Alithea is aware of Sparkish's unworthiness) and dismisses "honor" as "a disease in the head . . . that alwayes hurries People away to do themselves mischief," men to lose their lives and women their love.

Although honor has more meaning than Lucy admits, Alithea has indeed allowed social convention to exert too much force on her since she is about to sacrifice her life's happiness to a strained ideal. Moreover, her devotion to honor turns out to be, in part, a rationalization for a selfish motive. She finally reveals that she favors the fool over the wit because she fears that a wit would be jealous and domineering. He might interfere with her peace and liberty, even send her off to the country.[31] She could not control a wit, but she believes she could lead a fool where she would. Thus even Alithea does not want a marriage of equals. Like her brother, she plans to insure happiness in marriage not by trusting to the fair dealing of her partner but by finding one too weak to harm her.

Alithea's attitude results from the assumption, prevalent in her day, that wit leads a man to satire, captiousness, and suspicious prying and is incompatible with good nature and simple affection. As the preacher John Tillotson wrote, "By a general mistake Ill-nature passeth for Wit," since the "Wit of Man doth more naturally vent itself in Satire and Censure, than in Praise and Panegyrick." [32] Young Bellair, the only man in Etherege's *The Man of Mode* (1676) who is honorably in love and eager to marry, is described as "by much the most tolerable of all the young men that do not abound in wit." [33] A worldly lady in Rochester's "Letter from Artemisa" explains that a fool is a better husband than a wit because the wit is incredulous, fickle, and insistent on examining all a woman's imperfections; but "the kind easie Fool, apt to admire / Himself, trusts us." [34] Although Alithea would never be unfaithful, like the lady in Rochester's poem, she does think it would be easier to live as she likes if she has a fool to deal with. She has had ample opportunity to observe Pinchwife, who thinks his suspicion proves his acumen and knowledge of the world. She has mistaken Sparkish's easy manners and unconcern for good nature.

However, Harcourt's love and Sparkish's exhibition of malice ultimately convince her that her views were both shortsighted and unworthy: the best way a woman can insure her happiness is to marry a man she loves and respects—and to trust him to treat her decently. She cannot rely on a fool's pliability since, as Lucy says, "that easiness in [a fool] that suffers him to be led by a Wife, will likewise permit him to be perswaded against her by others." Alithea, cured of her overcynical attitude that marriage can be no more than making the best of a bad situation, draws the moral of her story:

I wish, that if there be any over-wise woman of the Town, who like me would marry a fool, for fortune, liberty, or title, first, that her husband may love Play, and be a Cully to all the Town, but her, and suffer none but fortune to be mistress of his purse, then if for liberty, that he may send her into the Country under the conduct of some housewifely mother-in-law; and if for title, may the world give 'em none but that of Cuckold.[35]

(Since only marrying a fool for liberty applies to Alithea's own case, Wycherley must have decided, rather confusingly, to take this opportunity to criticize ladies who married for any motive other than love and esteem.) Wycherley made clear that complacency and imperceptiveness are not to be confused with good nature; furthermore, unlike many of his contemporaries, he insisted in his works and demonstrated in his life that good nature is compatible with wit.

Alithea, though an intelligent and good woman, has been undesirably influenced by a foolish traditional conception of honor —that, having agreed to marry Sparkish, she must do so—and by the calculating attitude toward sexual relationships which prevailed in her selfish society. Yet, although Wycherley derided empty conventions and prudential scheming, he did not blindly admire the natural man. Margery Pinchwife, the foil to the characters corrupted by society, is ludicrous because she follows pure natural impulse in blissful ignorance of social expectations. The country-wife provides the standard of absolute naturalness against which the other characters' artificiality is measured, but she is not presented as an ideal.

IV *The Natural Woman*

Margery has the simplicity, the directness, the delight in novelty and sensual pleasure, and the good disposition of the natural woman, untainted by worldly wisdom and undistorted by social repression. On her arrival in London, she loves her husband, partly because she is instinctively attached to her mate and partly because it has never occurred to her that there are other possibilities. As Pinchwife thwarts her attempts to enjoy herself, she begins to rebel; and, as he becomes more cruel and accidentally reveals Horner's interest in her, she naturally begins to dislike her husband and to favor his rival. With the cunning of a cornered animal, she manages to send a love letter to Horner; but she has to depend on Lucy, the maid, for the more elaborate stratagems through which the affair is consummated. Her letter— "the first love Letter that ever was without Flames, Darts, Fates, Destinies, Lying and Dissembling in't"—is doubly comic: in its rustic honesty and in the implied contrast between this sincere expression of feeling and what any sophisticated Restoration lady would write. In view of the heroics which would normally be expected, the childish flatness of "let" my husband "not see this, lest he should . . . pinch me, or kill my Squirrel" [36] is both funny and touching

In the final scene, when all the other characters are entangled in artificial deceptions and embarrassments, only Margery is free to express her feelings openly. Too simple to understand the impropriety of what she says, and too grateful to omit doing Horner justice, she insists that she loves him, even though Pinchwife is standing by. It takes the combined efforts of seven people to stifle her declarations that Horner is, to her certain knowledge, a highly adequate male.

Innocent of hypocrisy and mercenary motives, Margery is indeed a better woman than the ultrasophisticated Lady Fidget, who is so artificial that she wants to regulate even illicit love affairs in terms of class distinctions. Margery's freedom from social constraint makes her refreshing in a world where everyone else feels the need to sustain a social role. Often her simple declarations have a certain truth, as when she cannot believe that a man who loves her will ruin her. In a sense, the "ruin" of which her husband warns her is a chimera constructed by proprietary males like Pinchwife for their own selfish ends. Unlike most characters in the play, Margery is capable of love (or at least of uncalculating affection); and she wants to express her love in the natural way—by living with Horner as his wife. Her belief that she can slip out of her marriage bonds is absurdly simple-minded in terms of social actuality; but in terms of nature it is right: the reason a man and woman live together in marriage should be because they love each other. Horner exposes social pretensions because he is so intellectually superior as to see through them; Margery exposes them because she is too naive to be tainted by them.

Yet the witless Margery, however appealing, is too crude to live in civilized society. She is, throughout, a "Dear Ideot" [37] and a figure of fun. Nor is Horner, who follows nature with more wit but equal lack of inhibitions, held up for unqualified admiration; if he were, Wycherley would not have represented him as such a drudge to such contemptible mistresses. Wycherley's ideal figures are Harcourt, the rake converted by love, and Alithea, the sophisticated lady who is aware of social conventions but able to transcend them in order to make a marriage for the right reasons.

In *The Country-Wife*, then, Wycherley acutely analyzed what was wrong with relationships between the sexes in his society. He laid bare the selfishness of the proprietary husband, the man absorbed in business, and the fashionably indifferent fop. He showed the sordidness of the rake whose love life consists of bedding as many women as possible—and of the ladies of quality who differ from prostitutes only in their hypocrisy. And he suggested what the relationship between a man and woman should be when Harcourt and Alithea make their own marriage, based on love and respect; they voluntarily regulate their natural physical attraction by the institution of marriage. Wycherley forcefully satirized jealousy and affectation, favorite butts of the age; and, more significantly, he suggested the base and ludicrous aspects of the Don Juan who was usually presented as ideal.

Although *The Country-Wife* is very much Wycherley's own in characterization and theme, he adapted material from Terence and Molière. As Horner indicates, the idea for his trick came from Terence's *Eunuchus*,[38] in which a young man pretends to be a eunuch in order to get access to a girl. It is significant that, while Terence's young man and a hero of Sedley's based on the same prototype (in *Bellamira*, 1687) used their disguise to rape a woman, Horner uses his only to gain access to willing partners.

Molière's *School for Husbands* (1661) and *School for Wives* (1662) both demonstrate the futility of trying to keep a woman faithful by forcibly restraining her. Sganarelle, the repressive guardian of *The School for Husbands*, unwittingly carries messages between his ward and her lover, just as Pinchwife does between his wife and Horner. However, Wycherley sharpened the satire by making Pinchwife contribute more actively to Margery's infidelity by his scheming: Pinchwife makes his own fate at every step, while Sganarelle is often the passive tool of the young lovers.[39]

In *The School for Wives,* a jealous guardian, obsessed with fears of cuckoldom, plans to marry a simpleton whom he thinks incapable of deceiving him. Arnolphe, however, is not an odious figure like Pinchwife: despite his complacent selfishness in bringing up Agnès with the sole aim of increasing her utility to himself, he does love her, mean well toward her, and hope for happiness with her. Molière does not make clear the hostility underlying Arnolphe's proprietary attitude; there is something more sinister about wanting to own one's wife than Molière implies. Wycherley's presentation of Pinchwife is more penetrating; his satire, more forceful.

Whether Margery is considered a more realistic or merely a hideously degraded transformation of Agnès depends on one's view of human nature. For Wycherley, nature meant honesty, uncouthness, and uncontrolled animality; for Molière, it meant artlessness and did not preclude modesty and sense. The natural impulse which educates Agnès is honorable love; the natural impulse which educates Margery is the sexual instinct. Certainly, Margery is a more amusing character; and she is more realistic in that she shows the negative as well as the positive effects of unsophistication.

Wycherley elaborated on Molière's theme by providing three men, instead of one, who are selfish in various ways. It is obvious that his play is more vivid and vulgar than Molière's; moreover, it is as crowded, rather than as selective, as possible. (English playwrights always added characters and incidents to Molière's plots because the English audience demanded constant bustle and variety.) *The Country-Wife* is also, I believe, more honest and meaningful than *The School for Wives.* While Molière focused primarily upon the unthinking selfishness of a mistaken individual, Wycherley boldly exposed that of a generally accepted social attitude. Instead of ridiculing a man for trying to make his future wife abjectly dependent on him by stunting her mind, Wycherley laid bare the shortsighted selfishness underlying the whole conventional view of marriage in his society—exploitation of women and the arrangement of marriages for mercenary reasons. Wycherley honestly showed what happened when marriages were arranged without regard to love, while Molière apparently did not criticize the system, even though it would have separated his true lovers except for an unlikely chance. Instead of proving, with the aid of a trite ending, the stock romantic credo that love conquers all, Wycherley showed concretely how love is won and destroyed. His treatment of right and wrong ways in love is more comprehensive and more penetrating than Molière's.

The Country-Wife happily combines the sophistication of Wycherley's age with his personal bent, wit and farce with moral significance. Wycherley was no longer writing comedies merely to amuse, for he had become a penetrating critic of his age and its values. But he was not a preacher: he presented his satiric butts—the degradation of contemporary sexual relationships and the emptiness of professed sexual honor—as objects of laughter, not of vituperation. His attitude and his characters are consistently comic. Unfortunately, his touch was not so sure in his next and final play, *The Plain-Dealer*,[40] in which he came close to identifying with his protagonist, Manly, a furious denouncer of his society.

CHAPTER 4

The Plain-Dealer

I Inconsistencies in The Plain-Dealer

WRITING his next play about a year later, Wycherley again turned to Molière and developed in his own way the theme of the Frenchman's Le Misanthrope (1666). Alceste, the hero of Le Misanthrope, is an intelligent, upright man who so loathes dishonesty that he insists on telling the whole truth on every occasion. He constantly gets into quarrels by doing such things as informing a marquis that his verses are execrable; and he despises his more balanced friend, Philinte, for complying with the ordinary forms of politeness. In love with Célimène, a charming lady of the court, he angrily repudiates her for enjoying the tributes of men whom he considers worthless; he insists that, if she has true love for him, she will care about absolutely nothing else. In the end, having rejected all society as unworthy, he retires from it. Molière satirizes both the insincerity of his society and the arrogant extremism of Alceste, who is so sure of his superiority to everyone else. The ideal he presents is Philinte, who is sufficiently honest to appreciate Alceste and to avoid gratuitous insincerity, and yet conforms to social custom, condones minor failings, and recognizes that the court of Louis XIV, whatever its faults, is greatly preferable to a desert.[1]

Molière's attitude toward Alceste is typical of his age, which expected people to conform to ordinary social convention because it lacked confidence in absolute ideals and considered collective wisdom more reliable than individual opinion. A person who set his judgment above society's, who took pride "that the World and I think not well of one another," [2] was regarded as ridiculously arrogant, even if his criticisms might be justified. Jonathan Swift, for example, ridiculed Gulliver at the end of the Travels for his devotion to impracticable ideals and for his conviction of his own superiority that prevents him from treating other people with civility. Shadwell's *The Sullen Lovers* (1668), an early adaptation of *Le Misanthrope,* represents social nonconformity as mere perversity. Stanford and Emilia, the sullen lovers, are discerning; but they are primarily comic butts—irritable, ungracious, and consistently ridiculed by their normally well-adjusted counterparts, Lovel and Carolina.[3]

When Wycherley turned the play into *The Plain-Dealer,* however, he only sporadically followed Molière's moderate and typically Neoclassical attitude toward the theme. His most significant changes are suggested immediately by the new names of the play and its protagonist: *Le Misanthrope* became *The Plain-Dealer;* Alceste, Manly. Initially, it is true, Wycherley presented Manly as a satiric butt, a man who carries good qualities to absurd extremes; however, he then made Manly not only a romantic hero with whom the audience is invited to identify but one whose inordinate demands on life are satisfied.

Manly, a sea captain, has just returned to London after having lost his ship through his daredevil courage in a naval engagement against the Dutch. As the play opens, he is attacking his visitor, Lord Plausible, for meaningless, indiscriminate affability:

Manly: Tell not me (my good Lord *Plausible*) of your *Decorums,* supercilious Forms, and slavish Ceremonies; your little Tricks, which you the Spaniels of the World, do daily over and over, for, and to one another; not out of love or duty, but your servile fear.
Plausible: Nay, i'faith, i'faith, you are too passionate, and I must humbly beg your pardon and leave to tell you, they are the Arts, and Rules, the prudent of the World walk by.
Manly: Let 'em. But I'll have no Leading-strings, I can walk alone; I hate a Harness, and will not tug on in a Faction, kissing my Leader behind, that another Slave may do the like to me.
Plausible: What will you be singular then, like no Body? follow [,] Love, and esteem no Body?
Manly: Rather than be general, like you; follow every Body, Court and kiss every Body; though, perhaps at the same time, you hate every Body.[4]

Manly finally pushes out Lord Plausible. He then rebuffs Freeman, his lieutenant, and Fidelia, a girl who, out of love for him, has disguised herself as a boy and followed him to sea. Unaware of Fidelia's sex, Manly scornfully dismisses her as a coward and a flatterer. Although Freeman proffers sincere friendship, Manly rejects him for not being absolutely honest in all social relationships. Manly is convinced that there are only two sincere people in the world—his fiancée, Olivia, and his friend, Vernish—and that he cannot be mistaken in their virtue. Finally, the litigious Widow Blackacre bursts in, dragging along her son Jerry, in order to subpoena Manly to appear as chief witness in her current lawsuit and to instruct him in what to say. Freeman starts to court her, because he regards marriage with a rich woman as his only route to a comfortable income.

In Act II, Olivia exposes herself as a malicious gossip and a hypocritical prude, in conversation with her cousin Eliza, Plausible, and the pertly sociable fop Novel. (Olivia is revolted by the obscenity of *The Country-Wife,* although, as it later turns out, she has no scruples about committing adultery.) When Manly brings the skeptical Freeman and Fidelia to witness Olivia's perfect fidelity, they find her abusing her fiancé heartily, with the help of Novel and Plausible. Discovered in her perfidy, Olivia brazenly turns on Manly and finally gets rid of him by admitting that she is secretly married to another man. However, Olivia is attracted to the "boy" Fidelia and encourages her to return.

Act III is set in Westminster Hall, where the Widow has forced Manly to appear as a witness. Manly reveals in soliloquy that he still desperately wants Olivia and, when Fidelia presses offers of help on him, insists that she go to Olivia and beg for an assignation. He also gets into three quarrels and two lawsuits, but he is learning to dissemble: not only does he conceal from Freeman his continued desire for Olivia but he gets rid of tiresome people by framing appropriate lies. For example, an officiously helpful lawyer soon disappears when Manly tells him he needs legal services in a charity case.

When Fidelia returns to tell Manly that Olivia has contemptuously refused him and tried to seduce her, Manly further exercises his new skill at dissembling in his scheme of revenge. He forces Fidelia to meet Olivia, intending to take Fidelia's place in the sexual act. While Olivia is awaiting Fidelia in the dark, her husband. who turns out to be Manly's supposed friend Vernish, unexpectedly returns; but she dexterously gets rid of him. Fidelia arrives with Manly, who goes into the bedroom with Olivia. Then he slips away, leaving Fidelia to make a second assignation, at which Manly will consummate his revenge by arranging to have witnesses. Having made this arrangement, Fidelia is caught by the returning Vernish, who, after satisfying himself that she is female, prepares to rape her; but she escapes.

Vernish looks up Manly in order to enjoy his misery at Olivia's betrayal; but, when Manly unwittingly turns the tables by gloating over his possession of Olivia, Vernish is compelled by his own false position to pretend he relishes the tale. By catching the Widow in the act of forging a deed, Freeman forces her to take care of him financially. Manly accompanies Fidelia to her second assignation with Olivia, but they are soon interrupted by Vernish. As Manly has arranged, Freeman, Plausible, Novel, Jerry, and the Widow burst in and find Olivia embracing Manly, whom she has mistaken in the darkness for Fidelia. Meanwhile, Vernish, who has revealed Fidelia's sex in a scuffle with her, is unmasked as the double-dealer he is. Novel and Plausible further humiliate Olivia by reclaiming jewels she had accepted from them under false pretenses, for she had been encouraging both of them with hopes of marriage. Finally exposed to everyone as a mercenary whore, Olivia rushes out in disgrace. Manly rewards Fidelia's devotion by proposing to her; accepts Freeman as a sincere friend, despite his compliance with the age; and becomes more or less reconciled to society.

Throughout Act I, Wycherley treats Manly as a sophisticated Neoclassicist would be expected to do by presenting him as a comic and decidedly unpleasant extremist. Manly's opening conversation reveals him diverging as far from the desirable mean as Lord Plausible does, although in a more honest and courageous way: he can see no middle ground between fawning on those he despises and insulting everybody he meets. His "a true heart admits but of one friendship," while a salutary corrective to the indiscriminate cordiality of Lord Plausible or even Freeman, is a ridiculous exaggeration. Manly is right in terms of abstract principle when he boasts, "Counterfeit Honour will not be current with me, I weigh the man, not his title; 'tis not the King's stamp can make the Metal better . . . your Lord [Plausible] is a

Leaden shilling, which you may bend every way; and debases the stamp he bears, instead of being rais'd by't." [5] But his insistence on displaying his contempt is more uncouth than honest.

Wycherley contrasts Manly with Freeman, the clear-sighted yet good-natured representative of the golden mean, whom Manly rejects for not being upright enough. Manly is convinced that everyone but himself, Olivia, and Vernish is capable of unlimited baseness. His boundless confidence in these two, which contrasts with his ungenerous cynicism about Freeman and Fidelia, clearly prepares for a comic exposure in the following acts. Manly's positive opinions prove to be ludicrously wrong, and Freeman underlines the point by quoting Manly's own words to him in derision. It becomes clear that only people dishonest enough to assume Manly's humor can please this pillar of honesty. Like all fools in Restoration comedy, he mistakes the surface for reality: Freeman's civility for insincerity, and Olivia's pretense of misanthropic honesty for virtue. He is, however, intelligent enough to learn from his mistakes. At the end of the play, he recognizes that he is not infallible, that he should judge people by their actions rather than professions which happen to accord with his humor, and that "a complier with the age" can also be a plaindealer and a true friend.

But the play cannot be interpreted as the education of a comic misanthropist. Despite Manly's final admission, his basic character and attitude remain the same to the end. While he has learned to conceal his feelings on occasion and to make use of people's weaknesses instead of merely raging at them, as when he peaceably gets rid of the lawyer in Westminster Hall, he remains sour and humorless, "cannot easily laugh," and finds pleasure only "in despising" people.[6] The important questions of whether Manly has learned to accept relative instead of absolute values and will try to adjust to society are left unanswered.

Whether or not Manly is supposed to be reformed at the end, the comic interpretation of his character ignores much of the play. Surely he elicits a deeper emotional reaction than amusement. It is not just that Manly has good qualities—for so has any comic figure seen in the round. Nor is it that he is allowed to voice true satire, for even the contemptible Pinchwife can rightly criticize a greater fool, Sparkish. It is the way Manly is presented:

he is given a moral stature and treated with a seriousness which preclude dismissing him as a figure of fun. While Manly is sometimes absurdly demanding of his fellow men, there are times when his longing and disillusionment are treated with complete seriousness. His retort to Olivia—"You have fitted me, for believing you cou'd not be fickle, tho' you were young; cou'd not dissemble Love, tho' 'twas your interest; nor be vain, tho' you were handsom; nor break your promise, tho' to a parting Lover; nor abuse your best Friend, tho' you had Wit" [7]—is no clamor for inhuman perfection; it is a plea for decency in a world of heartless hypocrisy and malice. As the quarrel scene progresses, one comes to feel with Manly rather than watching him critically. The predominant impression produced is not that of a fool who is having his illusions forcibly stripped away but of a trusting lover who is betrayed and exploited by an evil woman.

Manly's learning to dissemble in Act III, although in some respects the education of a misguided comic character, also suggests the tragic debasement of an idealist in a corrupt society. In the opening scene of Act IV, as Manly writhes with uncontrollable lust, brutally compels Fidelia to do his will, and insists on using the act of love as an expression of hatred, he seems quite thoroughly degraded. Fidelia's deadly earnest remonstrations with him force one to take his moral status seriously. His bed trick on Olivia could pass in the Restoration comic world, which allowed sex to be used as a weapon, but not in the heroic world into which Fidelia forces him, where love is pure and honor dearer than life; in the second context, he should, if not suffer, at least repent for his moral lapse.

Thus the comic butt of Act I has gradually become a serious hero. By Act V, although Manly has not changed, he is held up for almost unqualified admiration. His rigid principles have left him penniless and betrayed, but it is not clear that a more compliant spirit would have served him better. When Freeman finds it hard to believe that a man who has "oblig'd so many, can't borrow fifty or an hundred pound," Manly retorts that Freeman, with all his easy friendship and flattery, is in the same position. [8] Perhaps the plain-dealer is right after all, for he has at least kept his integrity. Manly is very sympathetically presented in his interviews with Vernish as a man who lives up to his high ideal of friendship, and he appears along with Freeman as a defender of values against the fops, discriminating skillfully between true and false wit.

The ending of *The Plain-Dealer* makes it impossible to view Manly as a mere satiric butt. If his denunciatory and uncompromising attitude is meant to be comically distorted, it should be exposed as false and impractical by the end of the play. But this exposure is not what happens. Manly demands unconditional and selfless love, exactly what he gets from Fidelia. When Alceste insists that Célimène demonstrate perfect love by going away to live with him in solitude, she sensibly refuses; and he must go alone. But Fidelia would follow Manly anywhere. Moreover, though unprovided with worldly wisdom, Manly acquires both a fortune and complete revenge on the two who have betrayed him. It is an ending for romance, not for the realistic comedy that Wycherley claimed to be writing: ". . . the course Dauber of the coming Scenes,/To follow Life, and Nature only means." There are satiric touches at the end—Manly regrets that he cannot make a big sacrifice by staying in the odious world for Fidelia's sake, Freeman quips that one quarrels with the world "only because . . . [one] cannot enjoy [it], as . . . [one] wou'd do," and Manly resolves to be more moderate in future. But these are not emphasized enough to modify the melodramatic denouement, to pull the play back to realistic comedy.[9]

While there have been various plausible attempts to provide a unified interpretation of Manly, they all achieve consistency at the expense of ignoring certain aspects of the play. Manly is treated too sympathetically to be the perverse "humourist" described by Alexander H. Chorney, the Jonsonian "humours" character of James David Lott, or the raging malcontent satyr of Rose Zimbardo. Manly is endowed with too much wit to be the self-deluded blunderer whom Norman Holland describes. He is neither purged of his "humour" (Lott), nor "educated" not to expect absolute truth in this world (Holland), nor condemned for succumbing to hypocrisy, the very vice he declaims against (Zimbardo). His attitudes are slightly qualified at the end of the play but are not transformed; and he is applauded and rewarded with the fulfillment of his romantic wishes.

On the other hand, he is treated too objectively—too often

criticized, ridiculed, and deflated—to be interpreted either as an alter ego of his creator (Bonamy Dobrée) or as a typical romantic hero of the time. John H. Wilson has pointed out that Manly resembles the protagonists of contemporary heroic drama in his pride and overmastering passion, his intolerance of others, and his conviction that he is justified in pursuing his aims regardless of circumstances. In addition, he is rewarded with the love of Fidelia, a character more appropriate to heroic drama than to comedy. However, there is an all-important difference: those heroes were presented for uncritical acceptance, while Manly is placed in a satirical setting which demands a critical attitude.[10] Wycherley seems to have been unable to make up his mind about Manly, with the result that he is not so forceful a character as he should be: he is neither a noble hero nor a satiric illustration of the folly and arrogance of rejecting society.

Freeman, on the other hand, is consistently, and effectively, characterized. In harmony with his society, Freeman makes the best of life as he finds it, uses fools for his diversion, and manipulates people to secure what he wants from them. But, unlike his prototype, Philinte, he does not represent the balanced ideal. He has been so perceptibly corrupted by his self-seeking, cynical society that he boasts that he never dares "give a Woman a farthing" lest she steal everything from him, and he is eager to marry the virago Widow Blackacre to provide himself with a steady income. Manly is right about the shabby shortsightedness of this plan: "Thy Creditors . . . are not so barbarous, as to put thee in Prison, and wilt thou commit thy self to a noisom Dungeon for thy life?" Freeman, "a Complyer with the Age," [11] is more sensible than Manly, since an attempt to revolt against one's age is apt to end merely in personal frustration. But Manly's unshakable adherence to principle and his love untainted by the profit motive sometimes make Freeman look a little sordid.

Wycherley was able to maintain Freeman as a consistent foil to Manly, but his empathy with Manly distorted his presentation of Olivia. At times, she is so clever that she realistically could delude an intelligent though unsuspicious man. She convincingly outmaneuvers the worldly Novel, Plausible, and Vernish as well as Manly. Unlike Novel, she has real wit, which

Wycherley used both to entertain in itself and to reveal her heartless eagerness to shine, no matter at whose expense. Just after Olivia, still posing as a strictly honorable person, has announced that she "cannot rail at the absent, to flatter the standers by," she joins with Novel in doing exactly that. Novel has come to display his wit at the expense of the friends he has just been dining with, but every time he starts a malicious simile she completes it for him. Since Novel has the malice but not the wit to expose characters accurately, Wycherley ingeniously achieved an entertaining scene by making Olivia supply the wit in her interruptions:

Novel: I have been treated to day, with all the ceremony and kindness imaginable, at my Lady Autums; but the nauseous old Woman at the upper end of her Table—
Olivia: Revives the old *Grecian* custom, of serving in a Deaths head with their Banquets.

· · · · · · ·

Novel: . . . she never counts her age by the years, but—
Olivia: By the Masques she has liv'd to see.

· · · · · · ·

Novel: Then, we had her daughter—
Olivia: Ay, her daughter, the very disgrace to good cloaths, which she alwayes wears, but to heighten her deformity, not mend it; for she is still most splendidly, gallantly, ugly, and looks like an ill piece of daubing in a rich Frame.

Olivia is so intent on displaying her wit that she is not even aware that she is interrupting. Later in the scene, when Lord Plausible defends Sir John Current as "a Man of unquestion'd reputation in every thing," Olivia retorts: "Yes, because he endeavors only with the Women, to pass for a Man of Courage; and with the Bullies, for a Wit; with the Wits, for a Man of Business; and with the Men of Business, for a Favourite at Court; and at Court, for good City security." [12]

Although Olivia emphasizes the worst in everybody, her criticism is penetrating, even of Manly. She has seen that he can be easily deluded through his pride: "He that distrusts most the World, trusts most to himself, and is but the more easily deceiv'd, because he thinks he can't be deceiv'd." With partial justification, she reduces his courageous independence to a "spirit of contradiction, for you dare give all Mankind the Lye; and your Opinion is your onely Mistress, for you renounce that too, when it becomes another Mans." She is incapable of appreciating the good in Manly, but she can criticize him more acutely than any other character can. Even Eliza, her right-minded cousin, admits that there is truth in Olivia's uncharitable pictures.[13]

But Wycherley's disgust with Olivia often carried him away, so that he made her dissimulation so inept that she could fool no one but a simpleton. Her repeated self-contradictions to Eliza, such as indignantly protesting her virtue right after confessing she had a lover in her room, are too glaring to be plausible or even funny. Eliza is not the only one who reacts with "Fie, this fooling is so insipid, 'tis offensive." [14] Apparently Wycherley could not bear to make her a true wit, the ideal of the age, even though to do so was the only way he could have saved Manly from appearing a comic dupe. Molière handled this situation much better, for his Célimène is witty and charming enough to keep an intelligent man in love with her against his better judgment.

Not only is Olivia inconsistently represented as both a consummate schemer and a poseur able to fool no one but herself, but she is given lurid vices not appropriate in social comedy. Her hypocritical prudery, coldhearted coquetry, and use of sex for profit fit in the comedy-of-manners world; but her raw lust does not. The Olivia who cannot look at china without thinking of Mr. Horner's is an effective butt for social satire; the Olivia who practically rapes Fidelia belongs in sermon or heroic drama. Her clutching of Fidelia (smothering "with a thousand tasteless Kisses" a victim who "fenced with her eager Arms, as you [Manly] did with the grapples of the Enemy's Fireship; and nothing but cutting 'em off, cou'd have freed me") and Manly's reaction (Her lips "are such I cou'd still kiss,—grow to—and then tear off with my teeth, grind 'em into mammocks, and spit 'em into her Cuckolds face")[15] are too violent and too savagely expressed for a comic criticism of society. Olivia's attack on Fidelia is not only out of character, for in general she is governed by calculating self-interest, but is too extreme to have any point as social satire.

These inconsistencies can be explained only as the result of a blurring of artistic purpose—caused by an unconscious discrepancy between what Wycherley had aimed to do and what part of his nature compelled him to do. He revealed some confusion about his aims even in his strangely inappropriate choice of an epigraph for the play, the Horatian "Ridicule commonly decides great matters more forcibly and better than severity." What was apparently intended to be ridicule turned into something deeper, more earnest, more violent.

Probably, inspired by *Le Misanthrope*, Wycherley had originally planned to show the baseness of society by letting an extremist measure it against absolute moral standards and, at the same time, to show the folly of flinging oneself against socially necessary compromises and deceptions. He had used a similar plan in *The Country-Wife*, in which Margery's absolute naturalness brings out the artificiality of everyone else, while simultaneously demonstrating the inadequacy of naturalness in a social setting. Such a scheme would require Wycherley to treat all his characters with detached amusement. Even when he exposed depravity, as in the Widow Blackacre's scene with her hired false witnesses, he would retain his sense of humor. The reader can laugh at the paradox that the Widow is honest since she pays people for perjuring themselves, for he is not emotionally involved with these characters and no direct appeal is made to his moral judgment. In order to satirize the two extremes of oversocialized and antisocial man, Wycherley would have to accept as his standard the best moral level that his society offered: Freeman's decent expediency would be the norm, and the expectation of anything higher than this norm would be folly.

Yet the conclusion seems inescapable that Wycherley was not satisfied with the norm. Into a world which recognized only Elizas and Olivias, Alitheas and Lady Fidgets, he introduced Fidelia, who obviously does not belong. While the most virtuous Restoration-comedy heroines wanted to be courted and appreciated and never forgot the prudence and artifice necessary to hold a wandering male, she has abandoned suitors and income to serve a man who brutally ignores her feelings and is prepared to follow him to the Indies, where wives "are forc'd / To live no longer, when their Husbands dye." Wycherley probably had in mind Dryden's *Aureng-Zebe*, produced the previous year, which is set in India and represents a virtuous injured wife, Melesinda, going off to commit suttee. Fidelia has the exaggerated self-abnegation of such pathetic ladies in heroic drama, and like Melesinda she is required to court her rival for the man she loves and is capable of taking pleasure in a kiss from him even though it is not an expression of feeling for her.[16]

The strained improbability of Fidelia results from the lack of confidence in lofty ideals characteristic of the Restoration, and her incongruous appearance in an allegedly realistic comedy represents Wycherley's personal ambivalence toward his age. Although in general he cheerfully accepted the standards of the court wits, Wycherley also felt a scarcely recognized longing for something higher. He probably saw himself as a man like Freeman—keenly penetrating into social pretenses, yet not indecorously upset by them; frank and loyal, yet not overburdened with moral preoccupations. Consciously he, like his characters Hippolita and Eliza, accepted his "pleasant-well-bred-complacent [complaisant]-free-frolick-good-natur'd-pretty-Age." [17] Like other sophisticated true wits of his time, he believed it naïve to expect people to abjure self-interest, extravagant to hope for more than sexual pleasure from love, and arrogant to require moral standards higher than those of the age. He thought that those who declaimed against the times were inspired by envy; they railed, therefore, against a society which, because of their own shortcomings, they could not enter.

On the other hand, Wycherley sympathized with idealism and questioned the worth of wit and expediency as the ultimate values. He sometimes suspected that the fascinating lady who charmed all the men was only "a mercenary Jilt" and that the apparent brilliance of the "Men of Wit, and Pleasure of the Age" was only tawdry glitter.[18] Doubting that genuine love between man and woman could really exist within the bounds of his society, Wycherley did not include a good realistic marriage in *The Plain-Dealer* to offset the selfish, mercenary sexual relationships of Freeman, Olivia, and Vernish. Instead, his only positive standard is an obviously unattainable ideal. Because of his disillusionment with Restoration society, Wycherley's sympathy shifted from Freeman, who adapts to the age, to Manly, who revolts against it: Wycherley ceased to see Manly as a ridiculous figure and was unwilling to dismiss him to a life of solitary misanthropy. Unable to solve Manly's dilemma within the bounds of realistic comedy, Wycherley resorted to the world of heroic romance for the unqualified ideal which Manly and he himself longed for: the ending of *The Plain-Dealer* is a wish fulfillment. To regard Wycherley as a misplaced romantic yearning for the Absolute would be absurd, but, in giving Manly a woman whose devotion was unqualified and untainted by selfishness, he surely betrayed a wistful desire for what his society did not provide.[19]

In *The Country-Wife* (with the possible exception of Lady Fidget's drinking scene) Wycherley kept these two sides of his nature in perfect balance: he represented both the sordid cynicism and the frank exuberance of his society; he showed Pinchwife's hatefulness but did not make the reader hate him; and he proposed a practical alternative to mercenary and faithless relationships between the sexes—all on a consistently comic and realistic plane. Wycherley's personal moral force is balanced against the tough-minded rationality and the detached mockery of his period.

In *The Plain-Dealer,* however, Wycherley's moral zeal overbalanced his social urbanity. Although he set out to strike a balance between the uncouth uprightness of Manly and the smooth insincerity of society, he made Manly into an almost tragic hero, who is disillusioned by an unworthy world and degraded by the corruption around him. Yet, lacking confidence in Manly's ideals, the playwright refrained from endowing him with nobility and sometimes even made a fool of him. The reader who starts to laugh at Manly's extreme ungraciousness or at his rigid refusal to compromise finds himself admiring this man whose moral principles place him unmistakably above his society. But once one starts to identify with Manly, he assumes so ludicrous or inhuman a pose that one recoils from him; one wants him to be noble and is constantly disquieted by his lapses. One's reaction to Manly is confused because Wycherley's own attitude toward him vacillated between detachment and identification. Molière saw good points in Alceste and at times sympathized with him, but he never lost his sense of humor about him. Wycherley presented Manly sometimes as a butt for satire and sometimes as a hero for uncritical sympathy.

The play is written, therefore, from two incompatible moral viewpoints and deals with two incompatible levels of reality. On the one hand, there is the ordinary attitude of Restoration comedy, based on cynical observation of life, that a sensible man should make the best of a society which is, after all, not so bad. Mingled with this attitude is the discordant view, based on the concept of some ideal world, that man should be more than a selfish animal, that he should try to approach absolute moral standards, and, consequently, that ordinary worldly behavior is despicable. Wycherley's inconsistency in attitude is manifested formally by shifts into (execrable) blank verse when he wants Manly and Fidelia to display their higher natures—self-sacrificing love or pain at practicing deception. Either level of reality could be accepted, but not both together. Drama cannot be fully effective when one's attitude toward the characters is made to fluctuate—nor can satire when faulty conduct is measured against shifting scales of values.[20]

II *The Theme of* The Plain-Dealer

The same uncertainty is evident in Wycherley's failure to define precisely the theme of *The Plain-Dealer*. A satiric play should explore a clearly defined subject, such as greed in Jonson's *Volpone*, sexual behavior in *The Country-Wife*, or the relationship between an upright man and a false society in *Le Misanthrope*. In *The Plain-Dealer*, Wycherley shifted Molière's emphasis from the evaluation of misanthropy to the social faults which produced it, partly because, identifying with Manly, he often looked through his eyes. Unfortunately (like Manly), he did not formulate clearly what he was attacking. If he intended to indict society as a whole, as Vernon believes, his error lay in choosing a theme so vast as to preclude a unified play. If, as is more likely, he meant to attack contemporary falsity, he included too much extraneous material, such as Olivia's lust; and he did not show a sufficiently close relationship among the various manifestations of falsehood in Restoration society—empty cordiality, hypocrisy, personal betrayal, perjury, and forgery.[21]

In spite of its blurred focus, however, Wycherley's attack on falsity is both forceful and highly relevant to Restoration society, in which declarations of love and friendship had degenerated into meaningless professions. It had become fatuous naïveté to depend on friend or mistress, or to trust anybody. Good manners were divorced from good nature and simply meant flattery of everyone, including those one will sneer at the moment their backs are turned. Lord Plausible stands out as a fop because his universal civility is clumsily exaggerated, not because it is insincere. Praise and detraction have become equally meaningless: "the absent think they are no more the worse for being rail'd at, than the present think they are the better for being flatter'd." Yet flattery is necessary for any type of success in the world. A captain must flatter some courtier if he wants command of a ship, no matter how fully he has deserved it by his services. A man must even flatter for a dinner: at an alderman's table, "you must call Usury and Extortion, Gods blessings, or the honest turning of the Penny." [22] Wycherley's picture is not greatly exaggerated: even Samuel Pepys, no rigid moralist, complained of the age because "a man cannot live without . . . dissimulation." [23]

Sickened by a society in which sincerity was stupidity and truthfulness ill-breeding, Wycherley confronted it with a hero who ruthlessly insists that every word be true, that every profession express genuine feeling. He contrasted Manly with Freeman, who is unusually honest and loyal for a normal member of society but also sees nothing wrong with hugging and flattering men and the next moment telling his friend that "they were Rogues, Villains, Rascals, whom I despis'd, and hated." [24] Below Freeman are people like Novel and Plausible, who are so insincere that they do not know what friendship is. Finally there are Olivia and Vernish, who betray the deepest commitments of love and friendship without shame or hesitation.

The Widow Blackacre and her law business help to develop this theme because the law, as Wycherley saw it, is institutionalized falsity. Though judicial processes were originally intended to illuminate the truth, they are now more likely to be an organized, seemingly respectable method for obscuring it. "The Reverend of the Law," Manly rightly charges, pretend that Westminster Hall is "the Palace or Residence of Justice; but, if it be, she lives here with the State of a *Turkish* Emperor, rarely seen; and besieg'd, rather than defended, by her numerous black

Guard here." ("Black guard" means literally menial or criminal attendants; symbolically, it refers to the black gowns worn by the lawyers.) Law in *The Plain-Dealer* is an instrument to help shrewd people, ones like the Widow Blackacre, to defraud their neighbors. In Westminster Hall, the Widow instructs three lawyers, all of whom assume that their function is to conceal the truth. Sergeant Ploddon does so by repeating the same thing over and over; Mr. Quaint, by decking her cause with flowers of eloquence, "that the Snake may lie hidden"; Mr. Blunder, by blustering so that his "own noise will secure" his "Sense from Censure." [25] Just as the jargon of the lawyers obscures sense and truth, the law itself obscures justice.

The Widow also uses legal jargon, but, unlike the lawyers, says what she means. This unabashed plain speaking, together with her tireless misdirected energy and the legal obsession which blots out everything else from her mind, makes her a richly comic character. She was undoubtedly modeled on Wycherley's father, who devoted his life to legal wrangling and who impoverished himself in his attempts to defraud his neighbors. He kept a reluctant son at legal studies, as she does her Jerry; and he no doubt would have regretfully acknowledged the truth of her allusion to "young Students of the Law . . . spoil'd . . . by *Playes*." [26] The case in which she subpoenas Manly concerns the rights of tenants when landed property changes hands—like the case which occupied Daniel Wycherley from 1673 to 1682.

When Freeman insists on courting the Widow Blackacre, she is exasperated not so much by his obviously mercenary motives as by his distracting her attention from business. She concludes her attempt to discourage him from fortune hunting, a wrangle as full of legal jargon and lacking in affection as a lawsuit: "Fie, fie, I neglect my Business, with this foolish discourse of love." When Freeman frees her son from her surveillance (in order to establish through him a hold on the Blackacre estate), she shrieks, "Why, thou Villain, part Mother and Minor!" [27]

Like most mothers, the Widow wants to protect her minor from wine and women, but she wants even more to keep him from legal action which might damage her interests: "O do not squeeze Wax, Son [set your seal to a legal document]; rather go to Ordinaries, and Baudy-houses, than squeeze Wax: if thou dost that, farewell the goodly Mannor of *Blackacre,* with all its Woods, Underwoods, and Appurtenances whatever. Oh, oh!" She has tender maternal pangs about his abandonment of his career—"Are all my hopes frustrated? Shall I never hear thee put Cases again to *John* the Butler, or our Vicar?"—but, when Jerry retorts that he has taken leave of "Pettifogging," she is so outraged that she declares he is illegitimate. She would rather proclaim herself a whore than let the estate go to an ingrate who disparages law business. Her obsession with the law so dominates every other feeling that, in the melodramatic scene when Olivia has just been disgraced by four men and is overwhelmed with shame and rage, the Widow notices only that they are making a seizure on Olivia's "Goods and Chattels, *vi & armis*", and she urges, "Make your demand, I say, and bring your Trover . . . I'll follow the Law for you." [28]

The Dedication of the play—to "my Lady B[ennet]," a noted procuress—reinforces Wycherley's attack on falsity. First, he ridiculed the shameless falsehood of contemporary dedications, which regularly consisted of flattering lies. The Plain-Dealer, on the other hand, told the truth to a patron from whom he could not possibly get anything. Second, he insisted that sexual relationships be given their proper names; for he equated Bennet's employees with upper-class mistresses who take their pay in presents and suggested that the matches she arranged might be less pernicious than the marriages conventional in society. Wycherley's main object of attack was ladies who, like Lady Fidget and Olivia, pretend to virtue by declaiming against honest representations of sex. At least Bennet was not a hypocrite.

III *The Reception of* The Plain-Dealer

The Plain-Dealer was produced on Monday, December 11, 1676,[29] with Hart as Manly, Haines as Lord Plausible, Mrs. Boutell as Fidelia, Mrs. Knepp as Eliza, Mrs. Corey as the Widow Blackacre, and Mrs. Marshall, a tragedienne, as Olivia. It is significant—presumably of Wycherley's intentions, certainly of the audience's reaction to the character—that Hart, the romantic leading man of the company, played Manly, since Hart would more likely have been seen as a hero than a comic butt.[30] At first, the Town was taken aback by the play, as well it might have been had it come expecting a jolly comedy which would bolster its complacency; the ladies in particular accused Wycherley of obscenity, though perhaps they were really protesting his outspokenness.[31] But, after the discerning critics—men like Dorset and Buckingham—had proclaimed "their loud approbation of" the play, "the Town fell Immediately in with them." [32] Dryden, too, publicly expressed his approval. In a preface of 1677, defending the usefulness and delightfulness of comedy and satire, he mentioned "particularly, the author of *The Plain-Dealer*, whom I am proud to call my friend," who "has obliged all honest and virtuous men, by one of the most bold, most general, and most useful satires, which has ever been presented on the English theatre." [33]

Indeed, Wycherley's contemporaries valued the play more highly than the twentieth century does. Everyone assumed that *The Plain-Dealer* was better than *The Country-Wife,* a judgment hard for most modern readers to understand.[34] Those who saw *The Plain-Dealer* in the theater must have been so carried away by the force of Manly, as played by Hart, that they were not aware of the inconsistencies which weaken the play. Discerning critics responded to its unmistakable moral force, which they considered a necessary qualification of serious literature and which appealed to their own taste for ruthless honesty.

Paradoxically, the Restoration, despite the prevalence of falsity, valued and in a way practiced plain dealing. Freeman, the complier with the age, is frank about his motives; and the clear-sighted Eliza speaks of "this Plain-dealing Age." [35] The Restoration wits were honest in their freedom from self-delusion, for, if they flattered and lied, they recognized what they were doing. The age compelled dissimulation and forced people to see that characteristic for what it was. For example, Rochester practiced and despised "the meane Pollicy of Court prudence, which makes us lye to one another all day, for feare of being betray'd by each other at night." [36] Halifax, who pursued titles and political preferment all his life, privately acknowledged that "A Man who will rise at Court must begin, by creeping upon All-four." [37] Men like these, loving the truth while knowing they themselves were false, would naturally admire Manly, who had the courage to express what they wanted but were afraid to say. They would feel that the main difference between him and them was that claimed in the Prologue to the play: Manly is "An honest Man; who, like you [the audience], never winks / At faults; but, unlike you, speaks what he thinks." [38]

The comments of Wycherley's contemporaries about plain dealing in general and this character in particular suggest that they regarded Manly as a predominantly admirable figure—brave, honest, and intelligent; imprudent, but not ridiculous nor unduly disagreeable. For one thing, no one expected a discerning person to be altogether good-natured, since he could not avoid being provoked by the folly around him. "Naturally *good Sense* hath a mixture of *surly* in it," Halifax wrote; "and there being so much *Folly* in the World, and for the most part so triumphant, it giveth frequent Temptations to raise the *Spleen* of Men who think right. Therefore that which may generally be call'd *Ill-Humour*, is not always a Fault." His advice that good sense "must be soften'd, so as to comply with that great beast the world, which is too strong for any man, though never so much in the right, to go to cuffs with," [39] implies that a person like Manly is theoretically right though is not, of course, to be imitated by one who wants to succeed. Congreve assumed that "a Splenetick and Peevish Humour," producing "a Satyrical Wit," portrayed things more judiciously than "A Jolly and Sanguine Humour." [40]

It is probable that what now appears as repellent harshness in Manly was not so unpleasant to his contemporaries. The similarity in tone between the court wits' own satires and Manly's diatribes suggests that they would have interpreted them as Manly himself does—as plain dealing. Dryden, who compared Wycherley's satire to Juvenal's, was typical of his age in preferring the savage Juvenal to Horace, whom he found urbane but insipid: "Juvenal is of a more vigorous and masculine wit . . . he drives his reader along with him." [41] Congreve in the Prologue to *Love for Love* (1695) deplored the passing of Wycherley's bold and violent manner in satire: "Since *The Plain Dealer's* scenes of manly rage, / Not one has dared to lash this crying age." [42] Wycherley's claim in his epigraph to be criticizing through ridicule rather than severity was not entirely the result of confusion in his purpose: "ridicule" was more "severe" in the seventeenth century than it is today.

Just as Manly's speeches are no more violent than contemporary satires, his actions are no more brutal than those of many sympathetic characters in Restoration comedy. Shadwell professed to be a moralist, yet in his *Squire of Alsatia* a supposedly honorable and amiable young man debauches an innocent girl while he is courting another woman to be his wife. In Sedley's *Bellamira*, supposed to be a satire on sexual licentiousness, an equally amiable young man rapes a virgin who happens to attract him; when, after discovering that her birth and fortune are suitable, he proposes to her, she and her brother accept him as an entirely desirable match. Audiences who appreciated these heroes would not find Manly's behavior especially brutal. At least Manly, like all admirable characters in Wycherley, refrains from harming innocent people.

Manly's immediate prototype, Alceste, was presented with amused detachment; but the Plain-Dealer was descended also from the bitterly satiric "malcontent" heroes of Jacobean drama, who were intended to be taken seriously. Malevole of John Marston's *The Malcontent*, for example, an honest but abusive declaimer against a vicious courtly society, is presented as an admirable and sympathetic figure. Apparently the original audience did not recoil from his unpleasantness as one does today. In the English dramatic tradition, the misanthropist-hero was a penetrating and upright man, one deserving respect.[43]

Without exception, contemporary references to Manly suggest that seventeenth- and early eighteenth-century audiences regarded him in the same way. Wycherley's friends at once took to calling him "Manly" or "The Plain-Dealer," and he felt complimented, as he obviously would not had Manly been intended as a dupe or butt. As late as 1733, although taste had become more refined, Pope wrote: "At half mankind when generous Manly raves, / All know 'tis virtue, for he thinks them knaves." [44]

His reputation assured by *The Plain-Dealer*, Wycherley was universally considered the greatest English writer of comedy since Jonson. He was admired not only for his powerful satire (reminiscent of Jonson), but for his "humours"—his creation of character. To Jonson, "humour" meant a trait such as greed which dominated a personality; by the Restoration, it usually denoted a distinctively individual character as contrasted with the stock social types who generally peopled Restoration comedy. The characters in the usual comedy of manners—the witty hero and heroine, the fop, the duped citizen—took what identity they had from social custom: the first pair had mastered the requisite social skills; the fop aped them unsuccessfully; and the citizen failed even to be aware of what was wanted.

The dramatist of "humours," on the other hand, was primarily concerned with the human character which underlay social fashions. When he dealt with greed, misanthropy, or litigiousness, he revealed universal characteristics which might be modified by particular social conditions but existed independent of them. Thus his characterization required more penetration into human nature and had more universal significance than mere portrayal of the upper-class social conditions of the moment. Unlike the manners characters, who tend to merge into one another even in the hands of good dramatists, a successful "humours" character stands out as an individual. "Humours," which should be both psychologically realistic and new, must consist of character traits, not merely of affectations or mannerisms of dress or speech.[45]

Although Dryden did not excel in creating "humours" characters himself, he acknowledged their importance in his criticism: "I approve most the mixed way of Comedy; that which is neither all wit, nor all humour [i.e., "humours" characters], but the result of both. Neither so little of humour as Fletcher shows, nor so little of love and wit as Johnson [sic] . . . I would have the characters well chosen, and kept distant from interfering with each other; which is more than Fletcher or Shakespeare did." Although repartee "is the greatest grace of Comedy . . . Yet . . . rather than all wit, let there be none."[46]

For this ideal the Restoration playwrights strove, and Wycherley achieved it more fully than any of the others. Etherege excelled in wit more than characterization; although Congreve recognized the importance of "humours," the outstanding merit of his plays is their wit; Shadwell created some effective "humours" but seldom attained wit. Wycherley's plays combine the wit and accurate social setting of the comedy of manners with the vigorous characterization of that of "humours." It was partly the strong impression made by his characterization of Manly and the Widow Blackacre that caused *The Plain-Dealer* to be esteemed above Wycherley's other works.

Wycherley's "characters are not rounded individuals," as Vernon has pointed out; but they "do not seem to be mere puppets . . . because their actions follow logically from the attitudes they hold." [47] That is, Wycherley analyzed human attitudes so accurately that the characters he built from them are realistic— they seem to live. Thus Pinchwife illustrates in every speech and action the results of regarding one's wife as a tempting piece of property, an attitude which developed from his blind selfishness and from his insecurity as a male. Wycherley excelled his contemporary playwrights in his grappling with reality—real human nature, as distinct from the social surface; real moral issues, as distinct from delicate social nuances.

CHAPTER 5

The Turning Point

I Marriage

AFTER the triumphant success of *The Plain-Dealer*, "The Satyre, Wit, and Strength of Manly *Wycherly*" formed the standard by which a rising young dramatist like William Congreve was to be judged.[1] For the rest of his life Wycherley was complimented as "Manly" or "The Plain-Dealer." He liked to refer to himself as "a Plain-dealer," [2] and he signed the Preface to his *Miscellany Poems* with this name. Alexander Radcliffe's semiderisive poem "News from Hell," which is knowledgeable and certainly does not flatter, confirms that Wycherley in *The Plain-Dealer* represented: " 'Bove all, his own dear Character: / And fain wou'd seem upon the Stage / Too Manly for this flippant Age." [3] Those who knew Wycherley must have been struck by a resemblance between him and his most famous character.

This comparison seems strange at first, for all commentators agree on the sweetness of Wycherley's disposition: "With all that *Severity* and *Sharpness* with which he appears on the *Stage*, they who were of his *Familiar Acquaintance* applauded him for the *Generosity* and *Gentleness* of his *Manners*. He was certainly a Good-natured Man." [4] "Mr. *Wycherley* was indeed of an affable, easie, good Temper, and perfectly inoffensive to all Company, and knew how to be Civil over a Glass to Mr. *Durfey* as well as to Mr. *Dryden*, but this was no mark of his Friendship or Intimacy." Although "No Man ever writ with more Wit or more Applause with the Judicious," "no Man ever assum'd less in Conversation on those uncommon Excellencies. He wou'd never be wiser than his Company." [5] His generosity and kindness gave him "a peculiar Distinction from ordinary Men of Wit." [6]

But Wycherley was like Manly in his outstanding sincerity and loyalty, qualities that were rarer than good nature among the Restoration wits. John Dennis wrote that sincerity was a virtue which had been "long and . . . peculiarly" Wycherley's own.[7] He "was as *Impatient* to hear his *Friend Calumniated,* as some People would be to find themselves *Defamed.*"[8] When the volatile duke of Buckingham was sent to the Tower of London for attempting to create trouble by forcing the king to prorogue Parliament on an obsolete statute (February, 1677), Wycherley strikingly demonstrated his loyalty. He wrote and circulated a poetic epistle to Buckingham which opened: "Your late Disgrace, is but the Court's Disgrace."[9] Considering that all Wycherley's hopes of advancement lay in the court, his tribute was a courageous one.

King Charles, however, forgave Wycherley's sally as he had so many by the court wits. When Wycherley fell seriously ill of a fever, the king visited him at his lodgings in Bow Street—a proof of "Esteem and Affection, which never any Sovereign Prince before had given to an Author who was only a private Gentleman." "Finding his Feaver indeed abated, but his Body extremely weaken'd, and his Spirits miserably shatter'd," King Charles gave him five hundred pounds for a journey to Montpellier, a noted health resort. So Wycherley went to France in the beginning of winter, 1678, and returned to England toward the end of the following spring.[10]

Unfortunately, Wycherley never fully recovered from his fever. It was probably encephalitis, an acute inflammation of the brain which often leaves permanent scars with loss of specific mental functions. His friends noticed how it impaired his memory, and it probably also weakened his creativity, judgment, and vigor. Dryden, writing nine years later to Etherege about his own apathy, casually mentioned symptoms which must have been generally apparent: "In short, without apoplexy, Wycherley's long sickness, I forgot everything to enjoy nothing—that is, myself."[11] Pope said that Wycherley forgot poems he had written two or three years before, so that he might "write one year, an Encomium on Avarice; (for he loved paradoxes) and a year or two after, in Dispraise of Liberality: and in both, the words only would differ; and the thoughts be as much alike as two medals of different metals out of the same mould." This memory loss was not the result of senile decay, for Wycherley had suffered from the same difficulty since the age of forty.[12]

What Wycherley's contemporaries described as loss of memory must actually have included a more complex change. Pope said that in his poems Wycherley "would repeat the same thought, sometimes in the compass of ten lines, and did not dream of its being inserted but just before: when you pointed it out to him, he would say, 'Gads-so, so it is! I thank you very much:—pray blot it out.' . . . His memory did not carry above a sentence at a time. These single sentences were good, but the whole was without connexion; and good for nothing but to be flung into maxims." [13] If the problem had simply been loss of memory, Wycherley could have recognized that the two thoughts were the same by reading over his poem. Evidently he had lost the ability to organize or concentrate sufficiently to produce a sustained, whole piece of work. Never again was he able to construct an effective literary composition—play or poem.

Wycherley must have seemed well on his return, however; for the king offered him the highly desirable post of tutor to his son by the duchess of Portsmouth, the seven-year-old duke of Richmond. He told Wycherley that he had resolved his son "should be educated like the Son of a King, and that he could make Choice of no Man so proper to be his Governor as Mr. *Wycherley;* that for that Service he should have fifteen hundred pounds a Year paid him," with a liberal annuity after his office terminated.[14] Wycherley's primary duty would be to impart knowledge of the world to his charge, to teach "skill in men and manners; pull off the Mask which their several Callings and Pretences cover them with, and make his Pupil discern what lies at the Bottom under such Appearances" [15]—a task for which the Plain-Dealer was peculiarly well suited. Wycherley seemingly was at last settled in the world, with the income that the other court wits had by their birth. Although the king's offer was particularly generous, a courtier of Wycherley's wit and charm, one who was a personal friend of the king and who had no independent financial resources, could reasonably expect to be rewarded in some such way.

After receiving this offer, Wycherley unfortunately took a trip to Tunbridge Wells, an elite resort, where "Constraint and formality are banished; intimacy ripens at the first acquaintance." [16] Walking past a bookseller's there with his friend Mr. Fairbeard,

Wycherley overheard "my Lady *Drogheda,* a young Widow, rich, noble, and beautiful," inquiring:

for *the Plain Dealer. Madam,* says Mr. Fairbeard, *since you are for the* Plain Dealer, *there he is for you,* pushing Mr. *Wycherley* towards her. *Yes,* says Mr. *Wycherley, this Lady can bear plain Dealing, for she appears to be so accomplish'd, that what would be Compliment said to others, spoke to her would be plain Dealing. No, truly, Sir,* said the lady, *I am not without my Faults any more than the rest of my Sex, and yet notwithstanding all my Faults, I love plain Dealing, and never am more fond of it than when it tells me of my Faults. Then, Madam,* said Mr. Fairbeard, *you and the* Plain Dealer *seem design'd by Heaven for each other.*

Wycherley took her home, began visiting her daily, and soon "got her Consent to marry her, which he did, by his Father's Command, without acquainting the King." [17]

Lady Laetitia-Isabella, countess of Drogheda, was indeed noble and beautiful, the daughter of the earl of Radnor and one of the leading beauties of Charles II's court; but she was not rich. She had been living on credit for months while she waited for her husband, the earl of Drogheda, to send her money from Ireland; she was constantly forced to financial expedients, including borrowing from her maid, Sarah Barnaby. Nor was she a widow when she met Wycherley, although she bought his picture, had his name engraved on a silver cup, and sent him a present of a diamond ring.[18] At the end of May, she returned to her husband in Ireland. The earl died in June, leaving all the Drogheda estates to his widow instead of to his brother, Henry, who would succeed to the title. When Henry contested the will, he maintained—justifiably, it would seem—that his late brother had been coerced by his wife and her relatives into bequeathing his estates out of the family.[19] In any case, although the countess was nominally rich, her entire estate, which was inherited from her husband, was now tied up in litigation.

When Wycherley secretly married the Countess, in September, 1679,[20] he could hardly have done anything more unwise. King Charles had offered the tutorship of his son to an unmarried man, who would be free to devote full time to his charge and perhaps take him traveling. Wycherley's marriage immediately afterward looked like contempt for the king's handsome offer. Moreover, it is likely that the king would have disapproved of a private gentleman's marriage to a lady with "a great Independant Estate, and noble and powerful Relations"; at least he should have been consulted, if only for the sake of etiquette.[21] Since news of the marriage was bound to reach the king eventually, the attempted concealment served no end but to exasperate him further. A man who accepted a position and then in effect rejected it by making a marriage which he knew would displease his benefactor, appeared to be more a double-dealer than a plain-dealer.

The marriage was equally unfortunate from a personal standpoint, for the new Mrs. Wycherley, who had a fierce, litigious temper, immediately embroiled her husband in lawsuits. Six months after the marriage, in 1680, the maid Sarah Barnaby brought suit for the money, which amounted to all her savings, that she had loaned Lady Laetitia. The Wycherleys could not pay her, for they had not yet received anything from the estate of Lady Laetitia's late husband, their only source of income. They fled to Ireland, and in January, 1681, Wycherley brought a cross-suit, probably under the goading of his wife. They were still in Ireland when the case was eventually heard in December. Barnaby won, and the Wycherleys were ordered to pay her debt with interest and all legal costs, amounting to more than three hundred pounds. They did not appeal the case, but absconded.[22] Wycherley's part in this affair is not creditable, especially on one occasion when, Barnaby becoming rudely importunate for her money, he beat her severely. On the other hand, his exasperation is understandable: he detested legal business, and the debt had been contracted by his wife, whom he had married in the reasonable expectation that her income would keep him free of financial wrangling for life.

Wycherley's verses "To my Lord Chancellour Boyle, at once Chancellour and Primate of Ireland: Written when the Author had a Suit depending before Him" express his state of mind during this dismal period as well as the cynicism about legal justice that he had shown in *The Plain-Dealer*. (These verses pertained to the suit over the contested will of his wife's late husband, which would be decided in Ireland. In this lawsuit Wycherley was, as he claimed, an innocent victim.) He praises Boyle for going against ordinary judicial practice "to be Just to Friendless Wit" and to uphold sense and innocence against law, "Since Reason o'er-rules Custom, in your Court." The author has "Marry'd, Richer, Happier to grow, / Which none sure, but a Fool, cou'd think to do"; and he asks Boyle, if he will not as judge decide for him in the Chancery case, at least as archbishop to dissolve his marriage:

> . . . since no Pact, or Bargain is allow'd,
> Without Consideration, to be good;
> And since 'twas an Estate, which in my Case,
> Consideration of my Marriage was.

Please, Wycherley concludes, "End my Law-Suit, or my Domestic-Strife." [23] Since Wycherley could not have married simply for money, King Charles having offered him an assured income, he probably meant that, while he had thought his marriage would more than compensate for the loss of the tutorship, it had in fact left him as financially hard pressed as before. He must have been bitterly chagrined to find himself immersed in legal squabbles and haggling with a servant. Like so many dupes in Restoration comedy, Wycherley had eagerly made what appeared to be a brilliant marriage only to discover it to have been a disastrous mistake.

Moreover, Lady Laetitia proved to be an insanely jealous virago. Aware of Wycherley's rakish reputation and disappointed in his sexual performance, she tried to keep him away from other women. According to Dennis, she: "was jealous of him to Distraction, jealous to that degree, that she could not endure that he should be one Moment out of her sight. Their lodgings were in *Bow-Street, Covent-Garden*, over-against the *Cock*, whither if he at any time went with his Friends, he was oblig'd to leave the Windows open, that the Lady might see there was no Woman in Company, or she would be immediately in a downright raving Condition." Wycherley "thought that he was oblig'd to humour" her, since she "had bestow'd both her Person and her Fortune on him." [24]

Several of Wycherley's poems seem to throw light on Dennis's rather mysterious account of the marriage. "To a Bridegroom, after having married an ill Wife to screen him from his Debts" probably describes the way Lady Laetitia acted when Wycherley wanted to go out:

With Jailers Questions, [she] still bars up your Way;
Where wou'd you go? and whom to see, I pray?
And if thou stir'st abroad, be sure that she,
To watch her Pris'ner, at thy Side will be.

Besides, he must "Toil in the Vineyard . . . [he] too rashly chose": "Constrain'd to Drudg'ry, each dull Husband beats / The Hemp of Wedlock in the Wedding Sheets; / And the gross Work of Love, in Form and Fear, repeats." That this was not just a conventional Restoration sneer at marriage is suggested by Dennis's hint that Wycherley was not able to fulfill Lady Laetitia's sexual expectations, either because of insatiability on her part or inadequacy on his. In another poem Wycherley complained that women's "constant Sensuality" causes males to "know no End of Drudgery." [25]

"To W. O. my Jocky-Friend . . . upon his Offer of a Wife to me" seems to be a fictionalized presentation of the reasons for Wycherley's marriage and of the nature of his wife's hold over him. Though the lady proposed by W. O. "has Two thousand Pound a Year, (you say,)," his peace, honor, and liberty are too great a price to pay for a wife and a fortune. Her title will not honor but disgrace him, for it will make her think she has the right to lord it over him; and her wit will only delude and enslave him. [26] The illusory fortune, the loss of peace and liberty after marriage, and the woman's title and consequent arrogance all fit Wycherley's relationship with his wife. He was a gentle, good-natured man who would rather give a woman her way than wrangle continuously, and his position was weakened by his consciousness of her social superiority and her greater physical vigor.

Mrs. Wycherley's jealousy had the even more serious consequence of keeping her husband away from court because she knew the likelihood of intrigues there. Good-natured King Charles might still have been reconciled, but Wycherley's failure to appear gave the impression that he was sullenly unconcerned to regain the king's favor. Perhaps, apart from his wife's scolding, Wycherley was ashamed to present himself at court; for he had reacted ungratefully to a generous offer, and he had made a marriage which was as disastrous to him as it was offensive to the king. And, of course, the longer he stayed away, the harder it would have been for him to reappear.

When Lady Laetitia died in 1681, she was generally unlamented. Wycherley recorded no tender reminiscences whatever of his married life. Although she left her whole estate to him, it was still tied up in litigation. Her family now held the Drogheda estates, while the new earl of Drogheda was contesting his predecessor's will. Wycherley brought suit against his late wife's relatives, but, since the property was so involved in legal complications, they found it easy to avoid disgorging anything.[27] Many years later—about 1700—her family, who still held her estate, paid him fifteen hundred pounds for his right in it.[28] Had this money been paid at the proper time, it would have spared him the misery of debtors' prison.

II *Destitution*

Meanwhile, Wycherley grew increasingly desperate, as his law costs mounted and he received nothing from his wife's estate. Finally, in 1682, he tried a direct appeal to the court in his *Epistles to the King and Duke* (of York). It is painfully obvious that the epistle *To the King* was written to bring the author to Charles's attention and regain his favor. Wycherley could find no better pretext than the indignation he claimed to feel at seeing libels against the king, which abounded because of the intense political bitterness and instability of the time.

The alleged Popish Plot had aroused violent anti-Catholic feeling, stirred up by the earl of Shaftesbury (Dryden's Achitophel). The Whigs, just forming as the party opposed to the royal prerogative, were trying to get Charles's brother, James, excluded from the succession because he was a Catholic, and had twice passed an Exclusion Bill in the House of Commons, though the Lords defeated the measure. A series of Parliaments were increasingly refractory, as Charles refused to cede his brother's right to succeed him. He did, however, send James out of the country while the agitation was at its height (1678-82). In 1681, Dryden had published *Absalom and Achitophel,* his great political satire against Shaftesbury and the Whigs. Predictably, Wycherley's *Epistles* express the same political views: "The Life of free-born Man is Liberty, / And Life of Liberty is Monarchy," since any other form of government means serving many masters instead of one.[29] This argument made sense to people who had experienced more tyrannical government under the Puritan republicans than under King Charles. Wycherley included a few biblical allusions in his poem and, like Dryden, described the English in terms of "the Jews."

Both Wycherley's epistles are long, rambling, repetitious, and difficult to follow. Wycherley had lost the ability to organize his material and the judgment necessary to prune what was extraneous or repetitious. He already showed the failing, which Pope was to remark on later, of unwittingly repeating the same ideas in similar words within the poem. For example, Wycherley, complaining that a poet cannot make his way at court, wrote that he is the "only hungry, ill clad, Flatterer." On the next page appear the lines: "Yet Poet, at *Whitehall,* sole Flatterer, / Who by the Rules of Court, is left to starve." [30] Wycherley's verse had always been prolix, for he had been too careless to polish it; but these repetitions, which were new, resulted from the brain damage caused five years before by his fever.

Of course it is no wonder that the poems seem forced, for Wycherley—unaccustomed to write of necessity—was grinding them out to save himself from debtors' prison. He never had been good at flattery; his forced efforts now were awkward and exaggerated. He tried to insinuate that he was out of favor only because he could not flatter at a court run by flatterers and, at the same time, induce King Charles to take him back on the grounds that "you hate Flattery, as you love Wit." Pursuing this subject, after several lengthy digressions, he told the king:

> You are sole Prince, who ever would decry,
> For Coin unlawful current Flattery;
>
> . . . .
>
> If counterfeiting Coin, we Treason deem,
> What is't to make a King quite other seem?
> If Treasons crime be Coins diminishing,
> What is't, to lessen, clip, wash o're a King?

The comparison between the false representations of flatterers and the false portrait of the king on a counterfeit coin is witty and ingenious, as are others in the poem; but—as is usual in Wycherley's later work—the witty idea is obscured by verbose development and slovenly expression. Finally, he described his own situation with tactful indirection: he is one of those bold poets who sue to the king "For promises, you gave to them ne're due"—the promise of the tutorship of the duke of Richmond, which was not due because of Wycherley's marriage. He begged Charles to forgive this lapse and to readmit him to his favor at court: "Worst crime is still, rejecting Heavens grace, / Worst punishment, is not to see Gods Face; / None wretched are, who can come where you are." [31] These lines show the adulatory tone of the epistle, though at this point Wycherley might have genuinely believed that all his troubles would end if he could regain the royal favor.

Wycherley's epistle "To the Duke" was ostensibly occasioned by his exile from the country during the anti-Catholic agitation. Writing to a less discerning recipient, Wycherley laid on his flattery more heavily by emphasizing the divinity of royalty and even by sinking to a comparison between "martyred" James and Jesus Christ.[32] Neither offering, alas, produced any response. Even if the royal brothers had been able to read through the poems, they were too involved in their own political troubles to worry about Wycherley's financial ones.[33]

All Wycherley had now were his own debts and those he had inherited from his wife. Mulgrave lent him five hundred pounds,[34] but that must have promptly disappeared in payment of court costs. Wycherley's poems to rich friends who kept him dangling in suspense about a vital loan or ungraciously boasted of their favors to him[35] may describe his mortifying experiences of this period. Finally, his creditors lost faith that he would gain anything from his lawsuit against Lady Laetitia's family; and, about 1682, they had him arrested for debt—a total of seven hundred pounds—and sent to Newgate Prison. He arranged his transfer to the Fleet Prison (a common procedure), where he was to remain for four years.[36]

It seems incredible that a man of Wycherley's attainments and social position could have remained in debtors' prison for so long, but actually squires, knights, even noblemen's children spent years there. Wycherley was penniless and had nowhere to turn for help—the king was disgusted with him, and his noble friends had evidently forgotten him. The circle of court wits had dispersed by this time: Rochester was dead; Sedley, retired to the country; Buckingham and Mulgrave, immersed in politics; and Dorset, recovering from a severe illness. Probably, too, the distinction between aristocrats and commoners, temporarily bridged when the court wits celebrated together, had reasserted itself. Aristocrats who let their one-time friend Butler die of want and who laughed when Dryden was beaten by hired hoodlums would not have worried when Wycherley was imprisoned.

Old Daniel Wycherley, who paid no attention to his son's plight, probably thought he was learning a valuable lesson about application to business: if William had known the law better, he might have been able to get hold of his wife's estate in time. Moreover, Daniel, involved as always in expensive litigation, had no money to spare for his improvident son. For some years, in fact, he had two sons in the Fleet Prison, William and George, his second son and a clergyman.[37] It is said that the publisher of *The Plain-Dealer,* even though he had made a fortune from the play, refused to lend Wycherley the small sum of twenty pounds.[38] Evidently Wycherley made no attempt to write his way out of prison, apart from his appeals to the king and the duke. Since a prejudice against "trading in wit" could not have lasted long in prison, it is probable that, as a result of his fever and his dispiriting surroundings, he found himself unable to create anything salable.

Debtors' prison was not so horrible to seventeenth-century people as it seems today. The Fleet, much the most comfortable of the prisons, has been compared to a shabby, overpriced inn. A prisoner could send for furniture, food, and drink from outside; tradesmen, including prostitutes, brought all sorts of merchandise in, and boys could be sent out on errands. A prisoner able to pay for it could have a room, or even a suite, to himself; he could bring in his family and servants and also receive unlimited visitors. There were usually two hundred prisoners in the Fleet, with double that number of wives, children, and servants.[39]

For penniless prisoners, whose wants were absolutely unprovided for, imprisonment was appalling; but, for the more privileged class (not so squeamish as one is today about crowding, dirt, and infectious disease), it was tolerable.[40] Some prisoners actually preferred to use their money to live comfortably (if expensively) in the Fleet than to gain their freedom by giving it all to their creditors or by selling part of their patrimony.

Wycherley, however, found life in the Fleet demoralizing and depressing. In his verses "In Praise of a Prison, call'd by its Prisoners their College; and written there," he ruefully acknowledged the follies which had caused his imprisonment—love (his marriage) and overconfidence in his business judgment. He alluded obliquely to his desertion by his erstwhile friends, who, the closer they were to him before, stayed the farther away from him now he was in prison. He tried forlornly to cheer himself with the paradox that at least he was now free from false friends and demanding women, but he could not rationalize away his depression: the occupants of the prison are "Carcasses of Skin and Bone, / From which, Life, Soul, Spirit, are dead, and gone." [41]

Charles II died in February, 1685, and was succeeded by his Catholic, absolutist brother, James. King James lost no time in antagonizing his subjects, among them Dorset and Sedley. He favored the prim Mulgrave, however, and on October 20 made him lord chamberlain, a post which gave him jurisdiction over the theater and, specifically, over plays given at court. Promptly, on October 24, Wycherley wrote Mulgrave a letter of congratulation from the Fleet, in a tone of dispirited obsequiousness which he tried desperately to disguise (from Mulgrave and himself) as witty courtliness. "Tho', amongst great Courtiers, the Congratulations of little and unfortunate Men are thought Compliments out of Interest, and rather a kind of giving Joy to their miserable little selves, than to their great, and successful Patrons," Wycherley began, "yet I assure you, my Lord, I congratulate your Lordship without any End by it, than appearing grateful to One, to whom I am so much oblig'd" (for Mulgrave's loan of five hundred pounds, which he had not been able to repay). Only then did he insinuate the real aim of his writing: that he would like to be received at court again.[42] This letter makes a sad contrast to the friendly communication between equals in Wycherley's other extant letter to Mulgrave, but it seems to have achieved its purpose of bringing Wycherley to official notice.

On December 14, 1685, *The Plain-Dealer* was performed at court. King James, who prided himself on his own "plain-dealing," "was mightily pleased with the play, asked who was the author of it; and upon hearing it was one of Wycherley's, complained that he had not seen him for so many years; and inquired what was become of him. The colonel [Brett, a friend of Wycherley's] improved this opportunity so well, that the king gave orders his debts should be discharged out of the privy purse." [43] He sent Mulgrave to find out the extent of Wycherley's debts. Unfortunately, Wycherley was ashamed to give the full list; he only mentioned the amount that would set him at liberty, so he continued to be harassed by creditors. King James not only released him from prison but allowed him a pension of two hundred pounds a year. [44]

About this time Wycherley was reconverted to Roman Catholicism. Doubtless it was his way of expressing appreciation to the king, who was zealous for the advancement of his religion and encouraged conversions. It was an easy change for Wycherley, who had before been a Catholic; and there was nothing else he could do in return for the king's generosity. He remained a loyal Jacobite all his life.

When Wycherley emerged from prison, he had lost his youthful gaiety and sprightliness. [45] But his wit and affable manners made him, despite his loss of memory and vigor, an attractive companion. His wit must have survived the impairment of other mental faculties, for discerning friends paid tributes to it which cannot be dismissed as empty compliments. Dryden would not try to dissuade a friend from marriage, "For having had the Honour to see my Dear Friend Wycherly's Letter to him on that occasion, I find nothing to be added or amended. But as well as I love Mr. Wycherly, I confess I love my self so well, that I will not shew how much I am inferiour to him in Wit and Judgment; by undertaking any thing after him." Wycherley, he observed, "has been a Batchelor, and Marry'd man, and is now a Widower. . . . Yet I suppose he will not give any large commendations to his middle State." [46]

John Dennis, who knew Wycherley only in later life, wrote to him: "You never are Witty to please your self, to whom Wit has so long been habitual, that you are often hardly mov'd your self when you say those admirable things with which we are transported." [47] Alexander Pope referred to Wycherley's outstanding "Wit, Probity, & Good-nature." [48] Dryden, Pope, and Richard Steele all quoted Wycherley's remarks, such as his opinion that Shadwell "knew how to start a fool very well; but that he was never able to run him down." [49]

III *"Wise Retreat"*

When James was driven from the throne in 1688, Wycherley lost his pension. He was left in the same position as his friend Dryden, who was also a convert; but he lacked Dryden's ability to support himself by his pen. At the time of James's abdication, Wycherley claimed that he had not ten pounds to bury his brother George, who had just died in the Fleet Prison.[50] Supported by what he could get from his father, Wycherley read, wrote occasionally, and discussed literature with his friends.

For the rest of his life, he remained in dignified retirement. Thomas Southerne, surveying the theatrical scene in 1693, on the occasion of Congreve's *Old Bachelor*, said that Congreve was clearly destined to be the successor to Dryden, since Etherege was abroad, Nathaniel Lee and Thomas Otway were dead, and Wycherley "in wise retreat, / Thought it not worth his quiet to be great." [51] During these years Wycherley spent as much time as he could in London lodgings, as much as he had to in Clive. His father, who lived on and on until 1697, evidently required his son's presence at intervals.

Wycherley made no secret of his feelings about his father's protracted life and niggardliness: Dryden referred to them in his "Discourse Concerning Satire," and Charles Hopkins, in a verse-epistle to Walter Moyle sending good wishes to his friends in London, included: "May generous *Wicherley,* all suff'rings past, / Enjoy a well-deserv'd Estate, at last." [52] But Wycherley never enjoyed the estate, for his father managed to trammel him even after he came into his inheritance. In 1696, worried that his improvident son would dissipate the hard-won family property after his death, Daniel Wycherley drew up a financial settlement which restricted William to the income of the estate, instead of letting him inherit it outright, as the eldest son normally would have. At the same time, Daniel consoled William by borrowing for his benefit one thousand pounds to pay his debts. But, when his father died a few months later, William was left with this debt and accrued interest, and a strictly limited income.[53]

Although Wycherley could live on his income, he could not pay his debts, as he was anxious to do before he died. He was soon on bad terms with his nephew, Daniel's heir, who refused to let him raise money by either selling or mortgaging any of the land.[54] A week after Wycherley's last trip to London, in 1715, he was imprisoned for debt at the suit of Thomas Barnes, a former servant, who claimed thirty pounds. He had to be helped out by his cousin, Thomas Shrimpton.[55]

Fortunately, Wycherley's reputation was so securely established that during his whole life he enjoyed high esteem in literary circles. His plays were frequently produced: *The Country-Wife* in 1676, 1683, 1688, 1695, 1701 (twice), 1702, 1704, 1709 (twice), and 1715 (four times); *The Plain-Dealer* in 1678, 1681, 1683, 1685, 1691, 1694, and 1698. It was produced once every year from 1700 to 1703, twice in 1704, three times in 1705, and four times in the season of 1715-16. Even *Love in a Wood* and *The Gentleman Dancing-Master* were revived, the first in 1694 and the second in 1693.[56] Wycherley's name constantly appeared as a master of comedy in the works of nameless hacks and great authors alike. Often he had the pleasure of seeing references to himself, such as this one in Dennis's *The Impartial Critick* (1693): "We have particularly a Comedy [*The Plain-Dealer*] which was writ by a Gentleman now living, that has more Wit and Spirit than *Plautus* without any of his little contemptible Affectations, and which, with the Urbanity of *Terence*, has the Comick force which" he lacked.[57]

Wycherley also, more surprisingly, retained his reputation as a moral writer. (It was the nineteenth century, horrified above all by plain-speaking about sex, that condemned Wycherley as the most immoral of Restoration dramatists.) Jeremy Collier, who bludgeoned all the playwrights with abuse in his *Short View of the Immorality and Profaneness of the English Stage* (1698), was almost gentle to Wycherley; for Collier evidently recognized his moral intentions. Although Collier was scandalized by Manly's disrespect for lords, he had to "own the *Poet* to be an Author of good Sense." [58]

Steele condemned most Restoration comedy as immoral; but, reviewing a production of *The Country-Wife* in *The Tatler*, he emphasized the moral of the Pinchwife story (though he did interpret Margery's adultery as "ruin and destruction"). Although Steele disapproved of Horner, he maintained that he had to be characterized as he was to be realistic: "To this only it is to be imputed, that a Gentleman of Mr. *Wycherley's* character and sense, condescends to represent the insults done to the honour of the bed, without just reproof; but . . . a Poet had at that time discovered his want of knowing the manners of the Court he lived in, by a virtuous character in his fine Gentleman, as he would show his ignorance, by drawing a vicious one to please the present audience." As this quotation suggests, Steele knew Wycherley personally. In *The Tatler* of April 30, 1709, he quoted a bon mot of Wycherley's on the "insects called Easy Writers": "That, said he, among these fellows is called Easy Writing, which any one may easily write." [59]

Wycherley spent much of his time at Will's, "the wits' coffeehouse," which in the reign of Charles he had visited with Rochester, Dorset, Sedley, or Etherege. Coffeehouses were much like clubs, where men went regularly to drink coffee and talk with their friends. Although they were open to everyone—lords with their stars and garters would talk familiarly at Will's with threadbare clergymen and hack writers—each coffeehouse tended to attract a certain clientele. Established and aspiring writers, wits and would-be wits gathered at Will's. Men passed judgment on every new play or poem, read and criticized each other's works, and debated critical questions. Dryden, who spent his afternoons and evenings at Will's, would sit in his accustomed chair, surrounded by the more distinguished wits, while others would come as near him as they could. Dryden's critical prefaces—incisive, mature, polished, and yet colloquial—suggest the quality of this conversation at its best. After Dryden's death in 1700, the major wits at Will's were Wycherley, Samuel Garth, William Congreve, Charles Boyle, John Vanbrugh, William Walsh, and Nicholas Rowe. Wycherley is described at this period as "one of the politest Gentlemen in *England*, and the most civil and affable to Strangers, especially to those of our Nation [French], for whom he has an Esteem; he is a little shy and reserv'd in Conversation, but when a Man can be so happy as once to engage him in Discourse, he cannot but admire his profound Sense, Masculine Wit, vast Knowledge of Mankind, and noble but easie Expressions." [60] A character in Charles Gildon's *A New Rehearsal* (1714) asks whether Will's still holds "its ground. And do men now, as formerly, become Wits by sipping Coffee and Tea with Wycherley and the reigning poets?" [61]

Wycherley's circle of acquaintance in the latter part of his life changed from gay rakes and court wits to private gentlemen, including both professional writers and cultured dilettantes. He must, however, have seen Dorset occasionally (who had also become more staid) because Dorset had Wycherley's portrait painted by Sir Godfrey Kneller in about 1705 to hang on the wall of the Poets' Parlor at Knole Park. [62] This fine portrait, done when Wycherley was sixty-five, shows him to be still handsome but prematurely aged: he looks seventy-five or eighty. It shows the same large eyes as the Lely portrait, although they now reveal more awareness and painful experience, and the same shapely nose and heavy chin, although the face looks longer because it has thinned down. It is a more interesting face than that of the Lely portrait, and a very sad one. [63]

By and large, however, Wycherley's friends were now those who drew their distinction from literature. He became closer to Dryden, who began to make frequent references to his "dear friend" Wycherley. Thus in a Preface of 1695, when arguing that a chorus is not desirable in tragedy, he cited Wycherley's opinion, probably expressed in conversation at Will's: Racine's *Esther* (1689) "was never intended for the public stage, nor . . . could possibly have succeeded there. Mr. Wycherley, when we read it together, was of my opinion in this, or rather I of his; for it becomes me so to speak of so excellent a poet, and so great a judge." [64] Dryden proposed that Wycherley join him in writing a comedy; but Wycherley, aware of his diminished powers, declined. [65]

Wycherley's new friends were men a generation younger than he. Congreve, who had dazzled the Town with his first comedy, *The Old Bachelor*, produced when he was only twenty-three, had immediately established himself with the wits at Will's. William Walsh, a minor writer and rather a fop, must have been brilliant in conversation, since Dryden called him "without flattery . . . the best critic of our nation." Walter Moyle, "a most ingenious young gentleman, conversant in all the studies of humanity much above his years," was another friend at Will's.[66] George Granville, Pope's "Granville the polite," was a good-natured poetaster who, in the reign of Queen Anne, became a prominent politician and a discerning patron of letters.

Another of the circle, Thomas Southerne, was, like Wycherley, a Templar and a playwright, one whom Dryden thought worthy of comparison with the Restoration masters. He enjoyed enormous success in the early 1690's with his sentimental tragedies *The Fatal Marriage* and *Oroonoko* and with his gross (though allegedly moral) comedy *Sir Antony Love*. Letters and occasional verse of the time indicate that Wycherley was enjoying a pleasant social life with these young men. One wit, writing wistfully from the country to his friend in London, pictures his happy meetings with Southerne, Moyle, Congreve, and Wycherley, "The best good Men, with the best-natur'd Wit." [67]

John Dennis, now remembered chiefly as the ridiculously irascible critic derided by Pope, was in the 1690's a promising young writer emerging as one of the prominent wits at Will's. Though touchy and suspicious, he was an intelligent and upright man, a thoughtful critic, and the respected friend of Dryden and Congreve, as well as Wycherley. He had first drunk "Captain Wycherley's" health in the 1670's while on a visit to London from Cambridge, and he must have got to know him by 1694, when he wrote to him at Clive. Dennis's letter is a highly complimentary effusion, written to impress, as would be expected from a beginning writer to "the greatest Comick Wit that ever *England* bred." [68] Wycherley responded promptly, and from then on they wrote regularly. Theirs was the typical artificial correspondence of the time, each party vying with the other in courtly compliments and in witty displays of antithesis, paradox, and similitude.

Once, when Dennis was suffering from a thwarted romance, Wycherley wrote to console him, reinforcing the usual Restoration cynicism from his own experience: "If you have been deprived of a Mistress, consider you have lost a Wife, and thô you are disappointed of a short satisfaction, you have likewise escaped a tedious vexation, which Matrimony infallibly comes to be, one way or another." He promised that, when Dennis returned to Town, "Your Friends will do any thing to root out the remains of your Passion . . . I will grow a good fellow, and venture my own health, for the recovery of your good Humour." [69]

Dennis had previously avoided telling Wycherley about this love disaster because "your portion of Melancholly is not so small, that you have need to be troubled with another Man's Spleen." [70] And in truth, despite his friendships and high reputation, Wycherley must have found his last years bleak. His poem "In Praise and Defense of Old Age" musters few arguments, despite his fertility of paradox on other subjects: the best he can say for old age is that it allays fear of death.

CHAPTER 6

Miscellany Poems

I *Wycherley as a Poet*

IN the early 1690's Wycherley decided to publish a collection
of his poems by subscription, then a common way for a
writer of reputation to gain financial support from the public.[1]
He was probably also motivated by a pathetic desire to revive
his literary fame. But Wycherley had never been a poet. His ear
for verse had always been undependable; as Harley Granville-
Barker pointed out, "And I must yet keep out of his sight, not"
could win a prize for the worst blank-verse line ever written.[2]
Even Wycherley's best verses, such as the Prologue to *The Plain-
Dealer*, were defective in technique. He seemed to believe that
witty sense, with some approximation of regular meter, was
enough. It was enough for the Prologue to an excellent play, but
not for a piece that was to stand by itself as a poem.

Wycherley's friends were loyal, however. Dryden wrote to
Walsh in 1693 that Wycherley's poems would appear in the fall;
that, "if his versification prove as [well?] as his wit, I shall believe it will be extraordinary"; and that "Congreve & Southern
& I, shall not faile to appeare before it & if you will come in, he
will have reason to acknowledge it for a favour." [3] Dryden's hint
that Wycherley's technique was inferior to his wit was a kind
representation of a crucial flaw in his poems, the substitution
of paradox and simile for felicity of language.[4] But poor Wycherley was to be caught again in the toils of "business." Samuel
Briscoe, the publisher who accepted his manuscript, advertised
it in 1696; but he neither published the book nor remitted to
Wycherley the money he had received in subscriptions. Wycherley sued Briscoe in 1700, and ultimately got back his manuscript.[5]

Finally, in 1704, the book appeared—an unusually large folio
published by C. Brome, J. Taylor, and B. Tooke and embellished
with a fine mezzotint of Lely's portrait of Wycherley—to which

Wycherley added the Virgilian motto "Quantum mutatus ab illo"
—how changed from what he was! Wycherley introduced his
Miscellany Poems with a series of sardonic jokes, which have,
alas, more truth than he realized. His *Errata* list started "In
General the whole Book: In Particular, . . ." He wrote his preface
"To my Criticks . . . Who were my Criticks, before they were
my Readers" and dedicated his book "To the Greatest Friend of
the Muses, Vanity." [6] The book was generally condemned, as—
unfortunately—it deserved. Poem after poem is merely a paradox,
ingenious but not sufficiently witty to stand by itself; versification is clumsy, syntax contorted; there is none of the neatness
which should grace comic or satiric verse; nor, indeed, is there
a single really felicitous line. Wycherley's poems were just not
worthy of publication.

The themes of the book, mostly Restoration commonplaces,
show no evidence of the original thinking of Wycherley's great
plays. For example, Wycherley argues that marriage is slavery,
taking all the pleasure out of love ("In Answer to a Mistress, who
desir'd her Lover to Marry her . . .") or that the brutes are superior to rational man ("Upon the Impertinence of Knowledge,
the Unreasonableness of Reason, and the Brutality of Humanity").
The latter poem develops the same theme as Rochester's "A
Satyr against Mankind" and Butler's "Satire in Two Parts, Upon
the Imperfection and Abuse of Human Learning." Wycherley's
songs, hardly distinguishable from those of the other court wits
in style and subject, were probably written in the reign of
Charles II. For the most part, they are adequately versified and,
as Pope said, needed only to be shortened to be made presentable.[7]

With remarkably poor judgment, Wycherley made his selection of poems in accordance with Restoration taste. Although
there are some of the moral satires and stoical discourses appropriate to a formal collection, there are far too many erotic
poems, typically sordid and often obscene. Readers of 1704 were
understandably not interested in cumbersome epistles "To a fine
young Woman, who being ask'd by her Lover, Why she kept
so filthy a thing as a Snake in her Bosom; answer'd, 'Twas to
keep a filthier thing out of it, his Hand; and, that her Snake was
to play with, and cool her in hot Weather; which was his

Aversion" or "Upon a Lady's Fall over a Stile, gotten by running from Her Lover; by which She show'd Her Fair Back-side, which was Her best Side, and made Him more Her Pursuer than He was before." The very titles indicate the unwieldiness of the poems: tolerable perhaps as ephemeral epigrams arising from some occasion in Wycherley's love life, they are hopelessly unsuitable as long epistles in heroic couplets published by an old man in an expensive folio.

Moreover, Wycherley's loss of memory and constructive power is everywhere apparent. Some poems practically duplicate each other, such as two epistles to a friend who had sent him a witty letter, explaining why he had not answered it sooner.[8] The same arguments keep reappearing through the moral poems and satires, even, sometimes, within a single poem. None of the discursive pieces is clearly organized. Wycherley's "Preface," for example, consists of two endless paragraphs which ramble from subject to subject without transitions. The individual observations are good enough, but there is no connected argument.

There are refreshing flashes of wit every now and then, as when Wycherley wrote "Upon an Old Worn-out Picture of Justice, hung . . . in a Court of Judicature," "That in the Court, some Justice might appear, / Justice is still hung in Effigie there"; or, on epitaphs, that, "Since most Great Tombs their Little Guests belie, / With some such Libelling damn'd Flattery." Wit does not, however, redeem the poems as a whole, though they bristle with similes and paradoxes. Sometimes these devices are so contrived that they add nothing to the vividness or impact of a poem, such as Wycherley's comparison of the law to a weak second in a duel because it professes to help injured innocence but does not actually do so. Even when a simile is truly witty—such as, in the same poem, his comparison of law to war because it makes "Reason yield to Pow'r"—its effect is often dissipated by overelaboration: the law-war comparison is developed for forty lines.[9] As Dryden pointed out, Wycherley was apt to display more wit than was needed, though, he kindly added, "never more than pleases." [10]

Even in his plays Wycherley had seldom achieved the seemingly effortless repartee of "Easy Etherege." Instead, he excelled in weighted *double-entendre*, especially when it revealed truth about character or situation, as in the china scene in *The Country-Wife*. He used wit superbly to point his perceptions of comic incongruities in the life around him. But sometimes he went astray by straining for wit—contriving similes and paradoxes to display his cleverness, or piling them up for their own sake. Only when he was fully concentrating on expressing character through speech or on developing a situation through brisk dialogue could he avoid the temptation of labored wit. The wit in Wycherley's plays was not really excessive, but it might be forced and therefore obtrusive.

In *Love in a Wood*, Wycherley had not yet formed his distinctive style; in *The Gentleman Dancing-Master*, he depended for comic effect mainly on farcical situations, together with obvious *doubles-entendres* turning on dancing and sexual activity. The wit in *The Country-Wife*, which develops naturally from character and situation, is almost always felicitous, as when Horner punctures Pinchwife's bravado with one line. Occasionally, however, Horner speaks like this: "The word is, I'll marry and live honest; but a Marriage vow is like a penitent Gamesters Oath, and entring into Bonds, and penalties to stint himself to such a particular small sum at play for the future, which makes him but the more eager, and not being able to hold out, looses his Money again, and his forfeit to boot." This statement can be unraveled, but it is hardly worth the trouble.

By the time of *The Plain-Dealer*, Wycherley's predilection for overelaborate wit had become more marked. For example, one of Manly's similes is so strained that it baffles analysis: "There is yet this comfort by losing one's Money with one's Mistress, a Man is out of danger of getting another; of being made prize again by love; who, like a Pyrat, takes you by spreading false Colours: but when once you have run your Ship aground, the treacherous Picaroon loofs [luffs], so by your ruine you save your self from slavery at least."

Even when a speech is really witty, it may be clogged with overabundant examples and details, such as Manly's protest against remaining any longer in Westminster Hall:

to have a Rogue, because he knows my name, pluck me aside, and whisper a Newsbook-secret [taken from the newspaper; i.e., no secret] to me, with a stinking breath? A second come piping angry from the Court, and sputter in my face his tedious complaints against it? A third Law-Coxcomb, because he saw me once at a Reader's [legal lecturer's] dinner, come and put me a long Law-Case, to make a discovery of his indefatigable dulness, and my weari'd patience? A fourth, a most barbarous civil Rogue, who will keep a Man half an hour in the croud with a bow'd body, and a hat off, acting the reform'd Sign of the *Salutation* Tavern [which showed two men bowing], to hear his bountiful professions of service and friendship; whil'st he cares not if I were damn'd, and I am wishing him hang'd out of my way.[11]

Manly could have made his point—that people talk not to communicate sociably but to gratify themselves—with fewer examples; and he develops his fourth example with so much superfluous detail that one trying to follow it loses the point of the speech as a whole. Generally, however, Wycherley's wit in the play is controlled by dramatic function. In his poems, where this control was lacking, the wit is more forced and long-drawn, without being redeemed by the humor and characterization which keep one from noticing awkward expression in his plays. Moreover, even the wittiest thoughts and figures cannot atone for invertebrate construction and slovenly versification.

Pope's soothing comparison of Wycherley to John Donne was not completely inappropriate (apart from the obvious fact that Donne was a poet) since both sometimes mistook witty ingenuity for poetic intensity, and neither had Pope's concern for meticulous technique. Wycherley, who admired the unmusical Donne, condemned as stupid the idea that Donne and Cowley lacked an ear for verse. When Pope revised this poem, he deleted the lines praising the older poets.[12] Of course, standards of wit were changing from the ingenuity valued in Wycherley's youth to greater simplicity in the Age of Pope.

Probably the best work in *Miscellany Poems* is "Upon the Idleness of Business. (A Satyr.) To one, who said, A Man show'd his Sense, Spirit, Industry, and Parts, by his Love of Bus'ness." The paradoxes are not mere empty ingenuities, as in so many of Wycherley's poems, but striking statements which are, in a way, true. Wycherley is defending the court wit's attitude against that of the serious businessman (like Sir Jaspar Fidget), who is

sure that he alone is applying his talents meaningfully. The
theme is developed with the wit—that is, penetration and per-
ception of unexpected likenesses—with which contemporaries
credited Wycherley.

"Your Man of Bus'ness, is your idlest Ass," the poem opens,
because his hard won gains of wealth, praise, or power serve
only to make him want more. Though his "Bus'ness is, to gain
himself more Ease," he can never be at rest because he constantly
wants more than he has: "For as one Wave, another does succeed, / So the first Bus'ness does another breed." Hence, we

> . . . Life, in quest of Sustenance, destroy,
> Our Lives so, but against our Lives, employ,
> For Bus'ness lets none, Wealth it brings, enjoy;
>
> . . . .
>
> A Sign of Emptiness then Action is,
> Circular Motion causing Giddiness,
> For Bus'ness, active Idleness is found,
> Which weakens Heads, the more 'twou'd prove 'em sound.

"The Love of Bus'ness then . . . is rather Reason's Shame, than
Proof":

> Out of more Pride, to bear more Slavery,
> To lose, for more Sway, Life or Liberty.
>
> . . . .
>
> Their Wealth, Time, Life (their own not truly) so,
> Away, but out of Selfishness, to throw.
>
> . . . .
>
> Whilst Beasts are Drudges, but by Force alone,
> But only Man, of his Free-Choice, is one.

The paradoxes are true wit because they have truth: business is
often but idle activity; the man of business, though motivated
by self-love, is actually working for others rather than for himself; supposedly rational man does enslave himself to drudgery
as a beast never would. The poem shows shrewd insight into
human nature: even the most avid, striving businessman protests
that all he wants is to attain ease and peace, although the only
way he could really get them would be relaxing his pursuit of

gain. There are even some effective lines—"Bus'ness is the Bane of Active Life"—although the versification and phrasing are far from meticulous. One notes, for example, the expletives joining their feeble aid to the first couplet quoted ("For as one Wave, another *does* succeed . . .") and the excruciatingly unnatural word order of the couplet starting "Their Wealth, Time, Life." Wycherley did get his lines to rhyme and scan, but at such a price of awkwardness that the correctness hardly matters.

The poem sticks to its point, as the *Epistles to the King and Duke* did not. However, it suffers from the prolixity and repetition of all Wycherley's last work. The wave simile near the beginning of the poem continues for seven additional lines which add nothing to the meaning. The idea that business is active idleness, which has been quoted, is repeated twice: "Then Bus'-ness is Laborious Idleness" and "By Love of Bus'ness, idle Industry." The poem runs for six and a half large pages, and it would certainly be improved if cut to three.[13]

Wycherley put a hopeful note on the last page of his book, "The end of the First Volume." He soon set about collecting materials for a second volume, despite the failure of the first—trying to write new poems and rewrite old ones, including even some of those already published in *Miscellany Poems*. He still did not realize how bad his verses were and thought that, if only he could polish them a little, they would make a respectable anthology. He was soon to find a helper in this task.

II *Friendship with Pope*

In 1704, Wycherley made the acquaintance of Alexander Pope, a bright-eyed, crook-backed boy of sixteen, who had come to London with some conventional but technically brilliant pastorals. Pope eagerly attached himself to a man of Wycherley's eminence, and Wycherley, complimented by the adulation of a youth of obviously high talents, kindly introduced him into the literary world. He appreciated the merit of Pope's pastorals and sent them to Walsh; Walsh and Congreve showed one of them to the publisher Jacob Tonson, who thereupon wrote Pope a flattering letter asking to publish them. Wycherley took Pope about with him everywhere. Granville, inviting a friend to his lodging to meet Wycherley, mentioned that he might bring with him

123

"a young Poet [Pope] . . . whom he and Walsh have taken under their Wing."[14]

Wycherley contributed a great deal toward establishing Pope as a literary man by introducing him to the most influential critics and making his work known. For a youth who cannot have been very prepossessing, Wycherley's sponsorship must have been invaluable. Dennis and George Duckett, the probable authors of *Pope Alexander's Supremacy and Infallibility Examined* (1729), gave a hostile but partially accurate picture of Wycherley's friendship with Pope in its early stages: upon Pope's "first coming to Town, out of pure Compassion for his exotick Figuor, narrow circumstances, and humble appearance, the late Mr. Wycherley admitted him into his society, and suffered him, notwithstanding his make, to be his humble admirer at Will's."[15]

Pope, in return, defended Wycherley when "the Town declaim'd against his Book of Poems." [16] In 1708, when John Ozell published a translation of Boileau's *Lutrin* which included a derisive reference to Wycherley's weighty volume of dull poems and a laudatory preface by Rowe, Pope composed an epigram against Ozell and Rowe and sent it to Wycherley.[17] When Pope dedicated his "Third Pastoral" to Wycherley, he commended his patron's sense, humor, judgment, and knowledge of human nature. Wycherley wrote a congratulatory poem on the pastorals, which was published (after, probably, being polished by its beneficiary) in *Poetical Miscellanies: The Sixth Part* (1709).

The first extant letter of the Pope-Wycherley correspondence is a flattering one from Pope to Wycherley dated December, 1704. When Wycherley replied a month later, he apologized for the delay that he had "been so busy of late in correcting and transcribing some of my Madrigals, for a great Man or two who desir'd to see them." The letters of Pope and Wycherley—a typical literary correspondence of the time, full of extravagant compliment and self-conscious wit—are too artificial to reveal much of the feelings of either writer. Occasionally Wycherley did comment on the overeffusiveness of Pope's compliments, comparing one of his letters to an author's dedication, "written more to show his wit to the World than his Sincerity, or gratitude to his Friend . . . so that you have provok'd my Modesty ev'n whilst you have Soothd my Vanity for I know not whether I am more Complimented than abused; since too much praise turns Irony."[18] Pope deleted this paragraph when, years later, he printed Wycherley's letters to him.

In February, 1706, Wycherley thanked Pope for correcting his poem to Dryden, written about ten years before.[19] Dimly aware of his technical deficiency as a poet—but still resolved to publish another volume—Wycherley had asked his young friend to "polish" his verses. Pope agreed, and for several years he struggled to give shape to the shapeless. It is remarkable that this arrangement lasted as long as it did. Wycherley, an established author of sixty-six, could not have realized how worthless his poems were nor how irksome a task he was imposing on Pope. Although Pope loved to tinker with his own and other people's verses, he must have grown exasperated in his futile efforts to improve Wycherley's without entirely rewriting them.

Sometimes Wycherley seemed to realize the pointlessness of what he and Pope were doing, as when he aptly spoke of the "barren Abundance" of his verses. But, however discouraged and humble he felt, he insisted on pursuing his project. He was very grateful to Pope and touchingly confident that he could reform the poems.[20] Pope, meanwhile, did not wish it to be known that he was revising Wycherley's work, presumably because he feared the final result would throw discredit on him. He explained what he had done to Wycherley's poem on dullness: he had organized it neatly into sections and subsections; he had omitted thoughts which repeated "something in your first Volume, or in this very Paper"; he had contracted verbosity; he had added thoughts "where I thought there wanted heightning"; and he had corrected the versification so that "no Body" could "be shock'd at" it. The result is a clearly organized poem of the proper length for its content and with a definite conclusion. Wycherley thanked Pope profusely, but with an ironic innuendo: "for the pains you have taken to recommend my *Dulness*, by making it more methodical, I give you a thousand thanks; since true and natural *Dulness* is shown more by its pretence to form and method, as the sprightliness of Wit by its despising both." [21]

Pope's reply was devastating. He asserted that omission of repetitions had been "but one, and the easiest Part" of the task of making Wycherley's poems presentable, "there remaining be-

125

sides to rectify the *Method,* to *connect* the *Matter,* and to mend
the *Expression* and *Versification."* As for Wycherley's jibe about
dullness being methodical, wit was not just *"Fancy* or *Conceit,"*
but propriety, which requires exact method. If Wycherley did
not want to methodize his poems, he would do better to "destroy
the whole Frame, and reduce them into *single Thoughts* in *Prose,*
like *Rochefoucault,* as I have more than once hinted to you." [22]
Pope was right, but Wycherley must have been intensely morti-
fied to hear that his verses, built so laboriously, would be better
if stripped down to prose sentences. The correspondence shows
strain on both sides, as each man tried to conceal the hostility
he must have felt over the revision of the poems. Wycherley
swallowed Pope's devastating criticism of his work, while Pope
struggled to imply tactfully that the poems would remain worthless unless they were completely rewritten.

Pope was always worrying when Wycherley did not answer
his letters immediately. On one occasion, Wycherley delayed
because of an accident sustained on April 31, 1709:

when I came from the Painters Tavern, with one Mr. Balam [one of
the wits at Will's, whom Wycherley had known from the early 1690's],
who, being something drunker than I, (because he thought himself
sober,) wou'd needs lead me down Stairs; which I refused, and therefore, went down very well, but at the Steps, going into the Street, he
turn'd short upon me, to help me again from falling, and so procur'd
my Fall; for Balam turning back upon the Ass, not the Ass upon
Balam; he fell upon me, and threw me backward, with his Elbow,
in my Stomach, and the Hilt of his Sword, in my Eye, bruis'd me so
sorely, I was forced to keep my Bed, for two Days. [23]

Wycherley still enjoyed convivial evenings and still had his sense
of humor.

By 1710, Pope was again correcting Wycherley's poems, for
Wycherley definitely planned to print a second volume that fall.
He still thought that all that was needed was smoother versification, so he asked Pope to put "my Rhimes in Tune," so that "my
rough Sense may be the less offensive to the nicer Ears of those
Criticks, who deal more in Sound than Sense." Pope continued
to protest that he found revising Wycherley's poems a pleasant
task, but he also noted that he discovered even more repetition
in them than he had thought. Wycherley, who accepted Pope's

account of the many repetitions caused by the "want of memory" of which he was aware, pathetically claimed to dislike tautology above all faults, and insisted that he appreciated Pope's frankness. At this point he terminated their collaboration by asking Pope to return his papers, but there appears to be no ill feeling in the letter (April 27, 1710), the last one extant from Wycherley to Pope.[24]

Pope did not entirely throw away his efforts on Wycherley's verses, for sometimes Wycherley's ideas appear (much better turned) in his own; and the best example is the source of one of Pope's great lines. In the Prologue to *The Plain-Dealer* Wycherley had arraigned the envious small writers who "with faint Praises, one another Damn." The line is clumsy, but the idea it expresses is both witty and psychologically penetrating: a compliment can indeed be as maliciously intended as an insult, and more damaging. Pope used it many years later in his caustic portrayal of Addison, sitting among his coterie of witlings: "Damn with faint praise, assent with civil leer." [25]

In other cases the indebtedness is not so clear because, after 1705, any of Wycherley's poems might include lines by Pope. But it seems likely that in virtually all cases the ideas were Wycherley's (for he could still turn out witty ideas in his old age), even if the phrasing was Pope's. Some famous thoughts in *An Essay on Criticism* seem to derive from Wycherley's "To my Friend, Mr. Pope on his Pastorals." Wycherley tells his young friend that in his "Verse are found/Art strengthning Nature, Sense improv'd by Sound." He used the same dichotomy in the letter to Pope in which he sneered at the critics who prefer sound to sense. And, of course, Pope wrote in *An Essay on Criticism:* "The sound must seem an echo to the sense." The next eight lines of Wycherley's poem seem to have inspired Pope's satire in this passage on the poet who lulls his reader to sleep by writing smoothly but without a thought.[26] Contempt for smooth, empty versifiers was more characteristic of Wycherley than Pope, who may have developed his ideas on the subject through conversations with his older friend.

A coolness developed between the two men in 1710, but in the fall of 1711 a mutual friend reconciled Wycherley to Pope. They spoke of Pope cordially and often, and Wycherley praised Pope's newest poem, the *Essay on Criticism*.[27] After this praise, they apparently remained friendly until Wycherley's death, although there was less effusive cordiality and no more talk of collaborative revising of Wycherley's poems. They saw each other in Bath in 1714, on which occasion Pope described Wycherley to John Caryll, another mutual friend: "that old lion in satire . . . now goes tame about this town. . . . He that dares to despise the great ones of this age, to deny common sense to ministers of state, their small portion of wit to the poets that live by it, and honesty to the maids of fourteen, dares not refuse Mr. Caryll his due." [28]

Throughout the course of the friendship, one sympathizes with Pope for finding himself caught in the futile and thankless enterprise of polishing Wycherley's work. Wycherley was making immoderate demands. But one would sympathize more had Pope been more candid; he never stopped professing that he enjoyed the task, and only thought of giving it over because—he could not understand why—his criticism and drastic revisions displeased Wycherley. Pope had a mania for self-justification: he had always to be the warm, sincere friend; and if a friendship cooled, it had to be the other person's doing. His protests of loving regard for Wycherley and constant sweet reasonableness in dealing with him make one suspect that his conscience was not quite clear, that he perhaps felt guilty about not being more grateful and forbearing to his generous old friend. His elaborate self-justification in a letter to Henry Cromwell of October, 1710, in which he accused Wycherley of jealousy, shows an unpleasant eagerness to put the old man in the wrong. All the evidence—Wycherley's actions and the opinions of others—supports the truth of his declaration to Pope that "I have (from my long experience of the World) learnt, to be slow to belief, as to anger, who, rather, than be unjust to my Friend, by sensureing his Faith too soon, wou'd be treacherous, to my self, by believing my Foes want of Faith to me, too late." [29] Pope deleted this sentence when he published the letter, for no evident reason except that it contradicts his picture of a peevish, jealous old man to whom he was constantly exercising forbearance.

Meanwhile, Wycherley planned a second volume of *Miscellany Poems,* with or without Pope's assistance. He continued to write, and he published in 1707 some congratulatory verses to the duke of Marlborough (who had been one of his successors in the duchess of Cleveland's arms). He wrote an Introduction for the book, which wistfully concluded: "What I have produced of late Years, Want of Health, and too much Leisure must in part be answerable for: I made my Study . . . the Amusement of my Melancholly; and it cannot be wonder'd, if I should desire to cherish its Issue; for ill Authors, like indulgent Parents, are most fond of their weakest Off-springs; and therefore all are fondest of those begotten in their Age." [30]

All or most of the poems which he wrote during these years, and which were published in Lewis Theobald's (1728) and Pope's (1729) editions of his *Posthumous Works* (where the texts are mostly the same, although Pope claimed that his were more accurate), were revised by Pope; therefore it is impossible to be sure what is Wycherley's and what Pope's. Certainly they are, on the whole, better than the *Miscellany Poems:* Pope regularized the versification, eliminated flagrant repetition, and added occasional neatly turned lines and similes. Nevertheless, these poems do not significantly differ from those in the earlier collection.

Wycherley did take Pope's advice to reduce some of his poems to maxims in the manner of La Rochefoucauld: prose epigrams revealing some usually shabby aspect of human nature. They are shrewd, if not profound, and more verbally felicitous than his poems. Many of them are merely translations from La Rochefoucauld or other writers; others repeat each other or what Wycherley had written elsewhere; others are platitudes or empty similes. Some of the maxims, however, are penetrating and well phrased.

The Silence of a wise Man is more wrong to Mankind, than the Slanderer's Speech. (Number 112)
False Wits, as Bullies in Courage, aim at Honour more by another's Disgrace than their own Merit; and like Criminals, expose their Brethren but to escape Condemnation themselves. (Number 239)
Design and Cunning are admir'd 'till discover'd; but then, like Tricks at Cards, which seem an Art 'till known, they are found to be mere Trifles. (Number 252)

Adapting La Rochefoucauld's maxim that "friendship is just an arrangement for mutual gain," which expresses his usual cynical acceptance of human baseness, Wycherley implied, rather, that

129

men should strive for something better: "The Friendships we shew to our Acquaintance, are often more out of Love to our selves than the Persons we call Friends; and we do Benefits, as Usurers lend Money, not so much for the Borrower's Service as our own Interest, which is rather exacting a Kindness than doing one. . . . For if Friendship be but doing as we would be done by, 'tis Commerce, not Kindness; a bartering Trade, but no Generosity." (Number 276).[31] Unlike La Rochefoucauld, Wycherley implies that friendship can and should be something more than commerce, and he is indignant that it so often is not.

The most effective poem in the *Posthumous Works* is the bitter "The Court-Life. To a Friend, disswading him from attending for Places." Why should we call it ambition, Wycherley asks, to obtain a place at court, where we must act in everything contrary to our mind and heart, pursue those who shun us, and gain trust by parting with virtue?

> Where we must say as Great Fools say,
> Do what Great Knaves will have us do,
> That we for Wits with Coxcombs may,
> With Fools for Politicians, go?

Where we must rise and sleep at others' will, swallow insults to delight them, "And slight good Men to honour Ill"? Where, in short, we must "Make many Foes, nay be our Own,/To gain a Friend where there is none"? Wycherley's declaration that at court we "Must pass our Youth in real Pain,/For Ease in Age to hope in vain" appears to be a rueful epitaph on his own early ambitions. The whole poem is a caustic satire on the degradation and falsity of life at the center of power—even at the glittering court of Charles II. While Wycherley probably could not have produced this unassisted, even though his songs were much better than his discourses in heroic couplets, the ideas are those of the plain-dealer, who was doubtless writing from his own bitter experience.

The version which Pope printed in his edition of Wycherley's *Posthumous Works* illustrates Pope's revision, or further revision, of Wycherley's verse. He cut down the rather clumsy six-line stanzas to quatrains, eliminating lines which were all unnecessary except for the poignant autobiographical ones. He regularized the punctuation and smoothed several lines—usually improving but occasionally weakening them. Pope's "Most alien to the Mind and Heart" is better than Wycherley's "Which farthest are from Mind or Heart"; but Wycherley's "And must gain Honour by Disgrace" is stronger than Pope's "And aim at Honour, by Disgrace." [32]

Although Wycherley kept many of his friends until the end, the dismal processes of mental and physical decay moved fast. Pope told Spence that Wycherley could remember nothing and was habitually peevish, though he "never did any unjust thing to me in his whole life." [33] In Wycherley's last year, 1715, his servant deposed, he was "soe much decayed in his Memory & understanding that he would often" send the man on errands and, having received the answers back, send him again upon the same errands.[34]

When he arrived in London in 1715, Wycherley met a Captain Thomas Shrimpton, his nearest surviving relative on his mother's side. Shrimpton assiduously cultivated his acquaintance and finally proposed to introduce him to a young woman whom he could marry. Wycherley had been playing with the idea of a second marriage at least since 1709,[35] because it seemed to him, as to Freeman in The Plain-Dealer, the only way he could raise money to pay his creditors. If he took a wife with a large enough portion to cover his debts, he could recompense her with a jointure on his father's estate of four or five hundred pounds a year; for, although his father had willed the estate out of his control, he had left him power to settle a widow's jointure on it. At the same time, he could take revenge on the nephew who would not help him by leaving this yearly drain on his income. For a man with the Restoration attitude toward marriage, it was not a completely fantastic plan.

When Shrimpton found out about it, he saw his opportunity to recommend a young woman, Elizabeth Jackson (who subsequently turned out to have been his mistress); and he persuaded Wycherley to put into effect his half-jocular scheme and marry her, eleven days before his death. Pope, who visited Wycherley on his deathbed, was not surprised; for Wycherley "had often told me, as I doubt not he did all his Acquaintance, that he would Marry as soon as his life was despair'd of."

Pope saw Wycherley twice after this visit, finding the old man "less peevish in his Sickness than he used to be in his Health; neither much afraid of dying, nor (which in him had been more likely) much ashamed of Marrying," for he had "dreaded the ridicule of the world for marrying when he was so old." "The Evening before he expired," Pope went on, Wycherley made a last request to his young wife: "*My Dear, it is only this; that you will never marry an old Man again.*" Pope commented: "Sickness which often destroys both Wit and Wisdom, yet seldom has power to remove that Talent which we call Humour: Mr. *Wycherley* shew'd his, even in this last Compliment. . . . At least, our Friend ended much in the Character he had lived in." [36]

A few months after Wycherley's death and after his widow had married her former lover, Shrimpton, Wycherley's nephew sued to invalidate the jointure. The ensuing trial unearthed another, more sinister story. Wycherley's nephew tried to prove that Elizabeth Jackson and Shrimpton had collaborated to coerce Wycherley into marrying against his will. Wycherley's servant testified that Shrimpton had tried to break down the old man's resistance by taking him out night after night and making him drunk and that he had finally browbeaten him into consent by convincing him that he was penniless and that, if he did not marry, he could get no medical attention and would have to be buried by the parish.

Although the court decreed that Wycherley's marriage—and hence the jointure—was valid, his nephew had witnesses that the old man was coerced, while Shrimpton was unable to produce any convincing witnesses in his favor.[37] On the other hand, it seems unbelievable that Pope could have been completely fooled. Wycherley was *compos mentis*, relatively cheerful, and amicably disposed toward his wife when Pope saw him after the marriage. He could hardly have been so if he had been subjected to the protracted, merciless browbeating which the servants described. None of Wycherley's acquaintance, except the witnesses testifying for his hostile nephew in a lawsuit, had any suspicion that he was being maltreated.

It may be hoped that the servants exaggerated and that Wycherley was not aware of the extent to which Shrimpton was using him. Wycherley genuinely wanted to relieve himself of financial pressure and to revenge himself upon his nephew, and the marriage could have been a final sardonic commentary on legal processes and mercenary unions. Odd as it was, it would not have been utterly shocking to a former Restoration rake for whom marriage had no particular sanctity; he was making an honestly mercenary marriage, such as Freeman proposed to the Widow Blackacre, instead of one clouded by sentimental pretense. At least Wycherley probably came to believe that the marriage was voluntary on his part; if he did, Shrimpton's actual designs are unimportant.

Wycherley died on December 31, 1715, and was buried in Saint Paul's, Covent Garden, his parish church. Thirteen years later Lewis Theobald, who had acquired Wycherley's papers through being the attorney for Shrimpton, published his *Posthumous Works*. Pope, who considered himself the only qualified editor for Wycherley, produced a rival volume, called Volume II of *The Posthumous Works of William Wycherley*, the next year.

CHAPTER 7

Epilogue

W YCHERLEY'S reputation as a preeminent playwright remained established until the middle of the eighteenth century. *The Country-Wife* was produced regularly several
times a year from 1715 to 1723, when Mrs. Bicknell, a famous
Margery, died, and again from 1725 to 1747. In the season of
1725-26, it was acted at both playhouses, for a total of thirteen
performances. Its last appearance in unaltered form in the eighteenth century was in 1753. David Garrick's *The Country Girl*
(1766), a bowdlerized *Country-Wife* with the adultery removed,
became very popular in the eighteenth and lasted into the nineteenth century. The original play reappeared only in this century.[1]

The continuing vitality of *The Country-Wife* is indicated by
its lavish productions in New York City in 1957 and 1965. Although one critic did dismiss it as a "decrepit Restoration romp,"
all the others admired the play's brilliant wit, comic freshness,
and vivid, biting portrayal of society. In 1957 they unanimously
praised Julie Harris's performance of Margery Pinchwife, particularly in the letter-writing scene. She "is both innocent and
funny," wrote Brooks Atkinson. "Her concentration on the knave-
ries of the moment. . . . The scribbling, scrawling, squirming
are uproarious." "The silken insult" of Pamela Brown's Lady
Fidget was also admired. The production, however, suffered
slightly from the inability of most modern actors to make the
most of witty lines and from a theater too large to permit the
intimacy between actors and audience which Restoration comedy
requires.[2]

The same defects were far more apparent in the 1965 production, which, although handsome and conscientious, failed to project Wycherley's wit and humor. Much of his irony was lost by
flat delivery, and one critic suspected that there was "more
laughter on the stage than from the audience." Modern directors
of Restoration comedies often become so preoccupied with sur-

face manners that they fail to bring out the author's penetrating characterization and criticism of life, reducing the play to an empty exercise. Such diminution is particularly damaging to Wycherley's work. Nevertheless, despite the difficulty of recreating Wycherley's wit, irony and satire, *The Country-Wife* will doubtless continue to attract producers and audiences. Howard Taubman concluded his review of the 1965 production: "Even in a lackluster performance it is possible to rediscover laughter and refreshment. A cheer, at any rate, for Wycherley." [3]

Although *The Plain-Dealer* was still considered Wycherley's masterpiece, it was presented less regularly than *The Country-Wife*—four times in 1716, five in 1721, once or twice in the seasons from 1721 to 1727, between one and eight times in each season from 1732 to 1743. It may be that Manly became less of a hero in the eighteenth-century productions, since Barton Booth's interpretation of the role was one of the "remarkable Instances" of his playing "Parts of Humour." [4] Voltaire, in his *Letters Concerning the English Nation* (1733), describes Manly as a primarily humorous character, in contrast to his "wise and sincere friend" Freeman. Although Voltaire considered Congreve the greatest English comic writer, he greatly admired *The Plain-Dealer* for its wit and boldness and for the humor of the Widow Blackacre, "the most amusing creature and the finest character on the stage." [5]

The season of 1743 marked the last appearance of *The Plain-Dealer* in unaltered form, although a version revised by Isaac Bickerstaff achieved seventeen performances in 1765. The critics generally approved of Bickerstaff's moralizing of *The Plain-Dealer*, but they felt he had badly weakened its wit and humor. By this time, the great Restoration plays were condemned as immoral. The *Public Ledger* of September 25, 1765, declared: "Wycherley, Etheridge [sic], and their contemporaries, were possessed of parts rather brilliant than useful . . . hence decency and good sense were continually sacrificed to an ill-timed emanation of vivacity; and so an audience could be set in a roar with some sprightly sally of genius, no matter what became of their morals or their understanding." [6]

Wycherley remained a model of satire and humor for dramatists as long as the tradition of Restoration comedy of manners exerted any influence upon the theater. Richard Brinsley Sheridan imitated Olivia's backbiting scene in the scandalmongers' party in Act II, Scene ii, of *The School for Scandal.* Wycherley's characters inspired many of his successors: Vanbrugh's Hoyden in *The Relapse* and Congreve's Prue in *Love for Love* are less attractive versions of Margery Pinchwife. Oliver Goldsmith's Tony Lumpkin in *She Stoops to Conquer,* a rather engaging lout who manages to escape from his mother's domination, was imitated from Jerry Blackacre; like Mrs. Blackacre, Tony's mother keeps her son a minor in order to retain control of him and make herself appear younger. Congreve's Heartwell, in *The Old Bachelor,* shows how a man completely in tune with his society interpreted Wycherley's Manly.

As one considers Wycherley's life, as distinct from his works, one must agree with the comment of his friend Charles Gildon: "Mr. *Wycherley* was a Person who set out with all the Advantages of raising a Fortune, and making as considerable a Figure in the World as any Man, yet no Man improved them less to his own Benefit." [7] Wycherley himself attributed his decline to Fortune, who "(like all other Jilts,) leaves those in their Age, who were her Favourites in their Youth; which truth I my self . . . have experienc'd sufficiently." [8] Both were right: it was a combination of bad judgment and bad luck that made Wycherley's life a perfect illustration of the favorite Neoclassical theme of the vanity of human wishes. Although he started out with every advantage—good looks and good nature, charm, integrity, wit, genius, immediate professional success, and welcome into the highest circle of his society—the last thirty-five years of Wycherley's life were unhappy and empty. The decline of his powers, the disintegration of the brilliant court milieu in which he had flourished, and the sordid legal and financial troubles make a sorry close. Wycherley had pleasant friendships and established fame but no meaningful occupation.

The sad futility of Wycherley's middle and old age must be attributed in large part to the fever which damaged his mental faculties in his late thirties. It ruined his memory and probably impaired his judgment—one thinks of his marriage and his insistence on publishing his poems. Even more disastrously, it incapacitated him for effective writing. The debilitating effects of the fever were reinforced by the dilettantish attitude toward writing which Wycherley had acquired through his companionship with the court wits. The very social milieu which had helped to inspire the sparkle and polish of his plays was to weaken him by disparaging businesslike application. Etherege and Congreve also stopped writing in their prime for no apparent reason but aristocratic laziness.

The court wits who enjoyed inherited wealth and position maintained that writing was for diversion only, scorned painstaking application, and sneered at professionals who wrote for a living. Wycherley adopted their pose of carelessness, which helps to account for his slovenly verse writing, and their aristocratic frivolity, which kept him from developing the discipline necessary to one who writes for a living. His poem "Against Industry: To a Laborious Poetaster, who preferr'd Industry to Wit" expresses the typical court wit's attitude that "the Best Wit, as the Best Gentleman . . . for his Wit, or Money, takes least Pain." Carelessness is the greatest grace to wit, as to beauty; and literary fame, like love, is best acquired through indifference. Wit pursued as business is as discreditable to a wit as business itself.[9] Instead of training himself to write professionally, Wycherley depended on the court for support, a source which conclusively failed with King William, who had no use for wit and charm. Once Wycherley lost the possibility of court patronage, he was far worse off than such "traders in wit" as the derided "Poet Squab". Ultimately, his success at court undermined his ability to make his own way.

It was bad luck for Wycherley that King James lost his throne shortly after settling a pension on him, but it was Wycherley's own fault that he lost the favor of King Charles. Sometimes he seems to have been driven by a self-destructive urge, of which the most striking evidence is, of course, his ill-timed first marriage. Wycherley was not a romantic boy but an experienced man of thirty-nine, and he must have known that he was throwing away the king's promise of the financial security and independence from his father for which he had been longing for years. Yet he married—and married a woman so perverse that his life with her was a constant vexation. Why did he do it? In view of his disgust with the law and his inaptitude for legal

137

business, his constant involvement in lawsuits also seems to indicate that he sought trouble.

It is evident from the violence and inconsistencies of *The Plain-Dealer* that its author was not smoothly adjusted to his society, despite his social success and convivial enjoyment. There were times when he despised its falsity and self-seeking and longed for selfless, uncalculating love. He was too infected by contemporary cynicism to develop convincing ideals in his plays or to pursue them in his life, but he seemingly felt the lack of them and sometimes turned against his own halfheartedness. Disgust with self and with a society from which he cannot extricate himself is apt to drive a man, unconsciously, to self-destructive actions.

The ironic development of Wycherley's later years almost suggests the operation of a nemesis—as he brought to happen in his own life the very things he had despised or laughed at in youth. In *The Plain-Dealer* he had satirized the law's injustice and delays—and he himself was to be constantly embroiled in lawsuits and spent four years in debtors' prison because his wife's estate was tied up in litigation. Despising craftiness ("of all sorts of Wit, that which Men call Craft, or Cunning, is generally found amongst the Weakest Animals of Men" [10]), he constantly got himself into situations where he needed it. Just as the independent Manly cannot borrow from any one of his prosperous relatives or obligated friends to save himself from starving, Wycherley could find no one to save him from prison; he "experienc'd all that Baseness in his Relations, Friends, and Acquaintance against which the *Plain-Dealer* had with so much Warmth inveigh'd." [11] The satirist of "a Laborious Poetaster, who preferr'd Industry to Wit" spent his own last years forcing out verses like any hack. The satirist of mercenary marriages made a ludicrously mercenary one at the end of his life by marrying a woman he did not know for money, and then obligingly dying, like the old man referred to in *The Plain-Dealer*, who "dyes as soon as he has made his Wife a good Jointure." [12]

The pathos of Wycherley's last years, however, is irrelevant to his literary achievement. Introducing genuine moral feeling into the frivolous, heartless world of fashionable Restoration literature, he gave his plays a substance and significance unique in their period. Although several Restoration dramatists claimed to have a moral purpose, Wycherley was the only one with real conviction—with a genuine value for decent moral standards and a genuine loathing for heartlessness and falsity. The admirable characters in all four of his plays are capable of sincere and loyal attachments, and they never take advantage of innocent people. Wycherley did not feel any abhorrence for adultery, but neither did he present it irresponsibly as a source of carefree fun; it was justified when the marriage had become meaningless as a result of the selfishness, the failure to love, of one or both of the partners. Unlike Shadwell, who claimed to give moral substance to the comedy of wit, Wycherley presented his characters honestly and never palliated sadistic self-indulgence. Shadwell, who saw no difference between debauching a virgin and courting a dissatisfied wife, insisted on treating his selfish heroes sentimentally; he would undoubtedly have married off Horner at the end of *The Country-Wife* to a nice young lady with whom he had been "in love" all along.[13]

The great plays of the Restoration are all free of such sentimental dishonesty, but they often reveal a touch of complacency. Etherege's *The Man of Mode*, for example, seems based on the assumption that the Restoration man of wit and breeding represented the highest point of human development and that Restoration courtly society had achieved all that was worth achieving. Wycherley, on the other hand, could see that all was not well with his society. In Horner, he suggested its sordid side; and, through Manly, he exposed the insincerity and self-seeking which were covered by its affable manners.

Finally, and most important, Wycherley added a great comedy to our literature. The farce of the china scene, the wit of the clever characters, the uproarious mockery of human self-delusion, the cutting satire of selfish attitudes toward the opposite sex, the thoughtful comment upon a part of life which is as central in our own time as it was in Wycherley's, make his *Country-Wife* a masterpiece.

Notes and References

Preface

1. John Dryden, *Essays,* ed. W. P. Ker (New York, 1961), I, 139, 142.
2. Dryden, *Three Plays,* ed. George Saintsbury (New York, n.d.), p. 162.
3. *Ibid.,* p. 173.
4. Quoted by Montague Summers in *The Complete Works of William Wycherley,* ed. Montague Summers (New York, 1964), I, 47.
5. L. C. Knights, "Restoration Comedy: The Reality and the Myth," *Explorations* (London, 1946), p. 149.
6. George Etherege, *The Letterbook,* ed. Sybil Rosenfeld (London, 1928), p. 27.
7. George Etherege, *Dramatic Works,* ed. H. F. B. Brett-Smith (Oxford, 1927), II, 216. Dorimant is actually speaking of the illusions produced by love, but I believe a Restoration wit would be equally apt to apply the metaphor to any of the sentimental illusions which make human nature appear golden.

Chapter One

1. Howard P. Vincent, "The Date of Wycherley's Birth," *Times Literary Supplement* (March 3, 1932), p. 155; H. Ince Anderton, *Times Literary Supplement* (March 17, 1932), p. 202.
2. Samuel Garbet, *History of Wem* (Wem, 1818), pp. 68, 70-84; Richard Gough, *Antiquities and Memoirs of the Parish of Myddle* (Shrewsbury, 1875), p. 85.
3. John Dennis, *The Critical Works,* ed. Edward Niles Hooker (Baltimore, 1939-43), II, 409.
4. Gilbert Burnet, *Burnet's History of My Own Time,* ed. Osmund Airy (Oxford, 1897), II, 390.
5. Charles de M. de Saint-Denis de Saint-Évremond, *The Letters,* ed. John Hayward (London, 1930), p. 194.
6. Anne, Lady Fanshawe, *Memoirs* (London, 1830), pp. 188, 214. The reasons for identifying the attaché with William Wycherley are:

(1) William is not known to have been anywhere else at this time; (2) there seems to have been no contemporary "Mr. Wycherley" appropriate for this role; (3) Daniel Wycherley had been a staunch Royalist and was not the man to hesitate to ask for deserved recognition; and (4) William, with his French language and manners and five years of living near the Spanish frontier, was qualified for the post. See Willard Connely, *Brawny Wycherley* (New York, 1930), pp. 45-47a.

7. William Wycherley, *The Complete Works*, ed. Montague Summers (New York, 1964), IV, 248. Wycherley appears to have genuinely hated war; see *Works*, II, 255-57, III, 203-5, IV, 227.

8. *Ibid.*, II, 270, ll. 16-21. Most authorities agree that this was the battle in which Wycherley was involved, but Macaulay thought it was the victory of Prince Rupert over deRuyter in the Third Dutch War of 1672-74.

9. *Ibid.*, IV, 84.

10. George Savile, marquis of Halifax, *The Complete Works*, ed. Walter Raleigh (Oxford, 1912), p. 198.

11. Thomas Hobbes, *The English Works*, ed. Sir William Molesworth (London, 1840), IV, 32; *Selections*, ed. Frederick Woodbridge (New York, 1930), pp. 177n., 281.

12. Hobbes, *Selections*, pp. 303, 309.

13. Halifax, *Works*, p. 209.

14. Gilbert Burnet, *History of My Own Time*, ed. Osmund Airy (Oxford, 1897), I, 167-68.

15. Samuel Butler, "A Modern Politician," *Characters and Passages from Note-Books*, ed. A. R. Waller (Cambridge, England, 1908), pp. 1-4.

16. Samuel Pepys, *The Diary*, ed. Henry Wheatley (London, 1910), III, 313.

17. John Wilmot, Earl of Rochester, *Poems*, ed. Vivian de Sola Pinto (London, 1953), p. 29.

18. Gilbert Burnet's life of Rochester, quoted in *A Restoration Reader*, ed. James Holly Hanford (New York, 1954), p. 253.

19. This prank of Dorset, Sedley, and Sir Thomas Ogle took place at the Cock Tavern, where several scenes of *The Plain-Dealer* are set. This is Anthony Wood's version, from *Restoration Reader*, p. 268.

20. Sir Charles Sedley, *The Poetical and Dramatic Works*, ed. Vivian de Sola Pinto (London, 1928), I, 40.

21. Rochester, *Poems*, p. 136.

22. Pepys, *Diary*, VI, 359.

23. Rochester, *Poems*, p. 120.

24. Wycherley, "Upon the Tyranny of Custom," *Works*, III, 138.

25. Butler derided his contemporaries who took pride in being as extreme in sin as men under the Commonwealth had been in hypocrisy: they "Call heav'n and earth to witness how they've aim'd/ With all their utmost vigour to be damn'd." See Samuel Butler, *The Poetical Works*, ed. Reginald B. Johnson (London, 1893), I, 191.

26. Pepys, *Diary*, III, 313.

27. John Evelyn, *The Diary of John Evelyn*, ed. E. S. de Beer (Oxford, 1955), III, 505. To avoid confusion, I shall refer to noblemen and noblewomen consistently by the titles by which they are best known, rather than changing whenever their titles changed. Barbara Villiers Palmer, Lady Castlemaine, became duchess of Cleveland in 1670, and will be referred to as the duchess of Cleveland; Charles Sackville, Lord Buckhurst, became earl of Dorset in 1677, and will be referred to as Dorset; John Sheffield, earl of Mulgrave, became duke of Buckingham in 1703, but will be referred to as Mulgrave.

28. George Savile, marquis of Halifax, *The Complete Works*, ed. Walter Raleigh (Oxford, 1912), p. 193.

29. Roger North, *Lives of the Norths* (London, 1826), II, 164.

30. George Etherege, *The Poems*, ed. James Thorpe (Princeton, 1963), p. 40.

31. Halifax, *Works*, p. 198.

32. There is some question about the authorship of "Colin," but it is attributed to Dorset in *Poems on Affairs of State*, ed. Elias F. Mengel (New Haven, 1965), II, 168.

33. Antoine de Courtin, *The Rules of Civility* (London, 1703), pp. 31, 41-42. By 1703 the work was in its twelfth edition.

34. Pepys, *Diary*, I, 311-12, V, 6.

35. See, e.g., Rochester's "Upon his Leaving his Mistress" and "A Ramble in St. James's Park."

36. Dryden, quoted in John Harold Wilson, *The Court Wits of the Restoration* (Princeton, 1948), p. 90.

37. Halifax, "Advice to a Daughter," *Works*, pp. 393-97.

38. Sir John Reresby, *The Memoirs*, ed. James Cartwright (London, 1875), pp. 204-7, 216, 259-60.

39. Richard Allestree, *The Ladies Calling* (Oxford, 1673), Part II, pp. 20, 27.

40. Sedley, *Works*, I, 111, 119.

41. Etherege, *Letterbook*, p. 417.

42. Halifax, *Works*, p. 46.

43. *Ibid.*, p. 199.

44. Dryden, *Three Plays*, pp. 162, 172.

45. Letter of Nell Gwynne, quoted in *Restoration Reader*, p. 135.

46. Sir Richard Steele, *Tatler* #1 (April 8, 1709).

47. Alexander Pope, *Collected Poems* (London, 1924), p. 295.

48. *Covent Garden Drolery* (1672), ed. Montague Summers (London, 1927), p. 61.

49. Burnet, *History*, I, 166-67.

50. Pepys, *Diary*, VIII, 188.

51. John Milton, *Paradise Lost*, I, 490-91, 501-2, II, 109-10, 116.

52. John Bunyan, *The Pilgrim's Progress* (New York, 1964), pp. 84-85.

Chapter Two

1. William Wycherley, *The Complete Plays*, ed. Gerald Weales (Garden City, New York, 1966), pp. 21, 91.

2. *Ibid.*, p. 104. James Urvin Rundle analyzed Wycherley's indebtedness to Calderón in "Wycherley and Calderón: A Source for *Love in a Wood*," *Publications of the Modern Language Association* LXIV (September, 1949), 701-7.

3. Wycherley, *Plays*, pp. 36-39.

4. *Ibid.*, pp. 62, 67, 120 (note).

5. *Ibid.*, p. 32.

6. *Ibid.*, pp. 42, 68.

7. *Ibid.*, p. 20.

8. *Ibid.*, pp. 10, 100, 112.

9. *The London Stage 1660-1800: Part I: 1660-1700*, ed. William Van Lennep, with introduction by Emmett L. Avery and Arthur H. Scouten (Carbondale, Ill., 1965), pp. xliii, 181. Alexander Pope gave Joseph Spence a chronology of Wycherley's plays which seems very unlikely: that he wrote *Love in a Wood* when he was nineteen (1659), *The Gentleman Dancing-Master* at twenty-one, *The Plain-Dealer* at twenty-five, and *The Country-Wife* at thirty or thirty-one. See Spence's *Anecdotes, Observations, and Characters, of Books and Men*, ed. Samuel Singer (London, 1858), p. 121.
In addition to making Wycherley incredibly precocious, this story provokes the unanswerable question of why he kept the plays around for years before production. *Love in a Wood* includes references to the Great Fire (1666); to perukes, which became fashionable in 1662-63, and to the vest, first worn in 1666; and to guineas, first struck in 1663. See Summers's introduction to Wycherley's *Complete Works*, I, 17. It is unlikely that Wycherley would have inserted all of these references years after writing the play.
If Rundle is right that he "undoubtedly used the 1664 edition" of Calderón's *Mañanas de abril y mayo* for the main plot of *Love in a*

Wood ("Wycherley and Calderón," p. 701), he obviously could not have written the play before then. Pope's mistaken information can be easily explained. Wycherley's memory was so poor when he knew Pope that his dating of anything could not be relied upon, and he was doubtless stimulated to exaggerate his own precocity by Pope's constant boasts about his. I also doubt that *The Plain-Dealer* was written before *The Country-Wife;* see Chapter 3, note 40.

10. John Downes, *Roscius Anglicanus,* ed. Montague Summers (London, 1928), pp. 16, 17, 97; Thomas Davies, *Dramatic Miscellanies* (London, 1784), III, 262.

11. Pepys, *Diary,* IV, 242.

12. *Ibid.,* VII, 287.

13. John Dennis, quoted in John Harold Wilson, *The Court Wits of the Restoration* (Princeton, 1948), p. 146.

14. Wycherley, *Plays,* p. 6. It was usual to attend a play one enjoyed several times in close succession, thus picking up any wit one had missed the first time.

15. Anthony Hamilton, *Memoirs of the Comte de Gramont,* trans. Peter Quennell; introduction by Cyril Hartmann (New York, 1930), p. 253.

16. Wycherley, *Plays,* p. 28.

17. John Dennis, *Letters Upon Several Occasions* (London, 1696), pp. 17-18; Spence, *Anecdotes,* p. 215; portrait of Wycherley by Sir Peter Lely.

18. Dennis, *Critical Works,* II, 409-10. Spence gives a slightly variant account, derived from Pope (*Anecdotes,* p. 137). In essentials the stories are the same, but Dennis's account has more vividness and point and presumably came from Wycherley himself. Leigh Hunt, in the life of Wycherley in his edition of the works of the Restoration dramatists, describes the duchess coming to visit Wycherley in his rooms in the Temple dressed as a country girl. Unfortunately, this intriguing tale seems to rest on no authority whatever.

19. Dryden, *Essays,* II, 19-20.

20. John Dryden, *The Poems,* ed. John Sargeaunt (London, 1910), p. 56. Cf. Samuel Butler's character "A Duke of Bucks"; "On the Prorogation," *Poems on Affairs of State,* ed. George de F. Lord (New Haven, 1963), I, 182-83; Burnet, *History,* I, 182; and others.

21. George Villiers, duke of Buckingham, *The Works* (London, 1775), II, 192.

22. Etherege, *Letterbook,* p. 212.

23. Pope, *Poems,* p. 117.

24. Rochester, *Poems,* p. 115; John Sheffield, earl of Mulgrave, and duke of Buckingham, *The Works* (London, 1726), I, 71.

25. John Dryden, Preface to *The Assignation, Of Dramatic Poesy and Other Critical Essays,* ed. George Watson (London, 1962), I, 186-87.
26. Dennis, *Critical Works,* II, 410. In August, 1672, Wycherley witnessed a legal document for Buckingham. See John Harold Wilson, *A Rake and His Times* (New York, 1954), p. 214.
27. Spence, *Anecdotes,* p. 17.
28. George Granville, Lord Lansdowne, *Genuine Works* (London, 1736), II, 110.
29. George Granville, Lord Lansdowne, *Memoirs of the Life of William Wycherley, Esq.; With a Character of his Writings* (London, 1718), p. 21. (Actually only the *Character* is by Lansdowne; the *Memoirs* are by Charles Gildon.) Dryden, understandably angered by Rochester's poem, retorted against it in his Preface to *All for Love,* in which he implied that Wycherley was not a slow writer at all (*Essays,* I, 199-200). Nevertheless, Pope cited the hastiness of Shadwell and the slowness of Wycherley as a critical commonplace in *Poems,* p. 295.
30. Rochester, *Poems,* pp. 96-98.
31. Wilson, *Court Wits,* p. 189.
32. Rochester, *Poems,* pp. 104-5.
33. Wycherley, *Works,* II, 247.
34. Robert J. Allen, "Two Wycherley Letters," *Times Literary Supplement* (April 18, 1935), p. 257. In his *Miscellany Poems* Wycherley printed "An Epistle from the Country, to my Friend Sir C. S. in Town; in Answer to one of His, wherein He wonder'd, I did not Answer His last" (*Works,* III, 121-22). This elaborately complimentary epistle, which gives no significant information, may have been written at this time to Sir Charles Sedley, known to have been a friend of Wycherley's.
35. There is some confusion about Lely's portrayal of Wycherley. If Spence is right, Lely painted Wycherley when he was twenty-eight, that is in 1668 (*Anecdotes,* p. 13); and the frontispiece of *Miscellany Poems,* a mezzotint of the Lely portrait, says the sitter was twenty-eight. On the other hand, all authorities date the only extant Lely portrait of Wycherley, which is obviously the original of the mezzotint, between 1677 and 1680. The portrait, now in the National Portrait Gallery, could represent a mature twenty-eight or a young-looking thirty-eight; but the fleshiness of the face suggests thirty-eight is the more likely age. Probably Wycherley's memory again proved untrustworthy.
36. Lansdowne (Gildon, really), *Memoirs of . . . Wycherley,* p. 9. Butler's own character of "A Duke of Bucks" emphasizes the perver-

sity and inconstancy indicated by this story, although he makes no specific reference to it.

37. Sheffield, earl of Mulgrave, *Works,* I, 64.
38. Pepys, *Diary,* VIII, 17.
39. *London Stage, Part I,* p. 192.
40. Downes, *Roscius Anglicanus,* p. 32.
41. Anne Righter, "William Wycherley," in *Restoration Dramatists,* ed. Earl Miner (Englewood Cliffs, New Jersey, 1966), p. 110.
42. Wycherley, *Plays,* pp. 208-9, 212.
43. *Ibid.,* pp. 143, 191, 247 (note). Summers compares Wycherley's play with Calderón's in Wycherley, *Works,* I, 40-44.
44. For the girls' apprehensions of criticism, see Molière, *Dramatic Works,* trans. Henri Van Laun (Edinburgh, 1875-76), II, 24 and Wycherley, *Plays,* p. 220. D. Biggins has pointed out that the specific device by which Hippolita gets Gerrard to enter her window may have come from Jonson's *The Devil is an Ass.* See "Source Notes for Dryden, Wycherley and Otway," *Notes and Queries,* CCI (1956), 300.
45. Wycherley, *Plays,* pp. 131, 138, 155.
46. *Ibid.,* pp. 169, 220.
47. *Ibid.,* pp. 192, 230.
48. *Ibid.,* p. 236.
49. Charles Dalton, *English Army Lists and Commission Registers, 1661-1714* (London, 1960), pp. xxi, 120, 129, 170. Sir John Reresby described life as an officer under Buckingham (in 1666) in *Memoirs,* pp. 66-67. Winifred, Lady Burghclere outlined Buckingham's activities in *George Villiers, Second Duke of Buckingham* (New York, 1903), p. 276.
50. Wycherley, *Plays,* pp. 403, 436, 439, 476.
51. Dennis, *Critical Works,* II, 412.
52. John Stow, *A Survey of the Cities of London and Westminster,* corrected by John Strype (London, 1754), II, 667.
53. Wycherley, *Plays,* p. 256.

Chapter Three

1. *London Stage 1660-1800: Part I,* p. 227. Hart created the role of Horner; Mohun, Pinchwife; Mrs. Boutell, Margery; Mrs. Knepp, Lady Fidget; and Mrs. Corey, Lucy, Alithea's maid. Sparkish was played by a newcomer, Joe Haines, who was well known as a prankster and man-about-town.
2. Wycherley, *Plays,* p. 296.
3. *Ibid.,* pp. 329, 369 (note). F. W. Bateson believes that Mrs. Squeamish "is not yet in the secret" ("L. C. Knights and Restoration

Comedy," *Essays in Criticism,* VII [1957], p. 64), but it seems to me that, although both interpretations could fit, Mrs. Squeamish's interest is far too keen to have been elicited by real china. "Deny your china" seems to be a plain reference to Horner's pretense that he is a eunuch. Double meanings in her speeches, as well as Horner's and Lady Fidget's, greatly enrich the humor of the scene.

4. Bateson, "L. C. Knights and Restoration Comedy," pp. 65-66; Norman N. Holland, *The First Modern Comedies: The Significance of Etherege, Wycherley, and Congreve* (Cambridge, Mass., 1959), p. 77.

5. I believe that this is a more accurate formulation of the play's theme than Rose Zimbardo's theory that *The Country-Wife* is a Restoration dramatic adaptation of Juvenal's Sixth Satire. Juvenal's satire is an attack on women (particularly for lust), while Wycherley's is an attack on wrong attitudes toward love and marriage on the part of both sexes. Juvenal is furiously indignant over any lapse from (female) chastity, while Wycherley makes light of adultery. Juvenal is misogynistic, while Wycherley defends the rights of women. See Rose A. Zimbardo, *Wycherley's Drama* (New Haven, 1965), pp. 147-49.

It seems to me that P. F. Vernon is much closer to the mark in seeing *The Country-Wife* as a satire on the contemporary marriage of convenience. In his article "Marriage of Convenience and The Moral Code of Restoration Comedy" (*Essays in Criticism,* XII [1962], 370-87), although he perhaps exaggerates the morality of the comedies' presentation of sexual relationships, he rightly points out that they extol the marriage of love, entered into by the free will of appropriate mates, at the expense of the marriage of convenience, ill-matched and motivated by greed.

6. Wycherley, *Plays,* p. 286.

7. John H. Wilson, *A Preface to Restoration Drama* (Boston, 1965), pp. 155-56; Bonamy Dobrée, *Restoration Comedy* (London, 1924), p. 94; Zimbardo, *Wycherley's Drama,* pp. 89-90; Marvin Mudrick, "Restoration Comedy and Later," *English Stage Comedy: English Institute Essays, 1954* (New York, 1955), p. 106; Anne Righter, "William Wycherley," *Restoration Dramatists,* p. 112. Righter goes on to argue that *The Country-Wife* is nihilistic because the distorted Horner, "who flays romantic and social ideals," completely overshadows the positive ideal characters, Harcourt and Alithea.

8. Wycherley, *Plays,* p. 271.

9. Holland first suggested that Horner's maiming is not entirely pretended: "part of him has died" (*First Modern Comedies,* p. 75).

10. Wycherley, *Plays*, p. 137.

11. *Ibid.*, pp. 284, 289, 324.

12. *Ibid.*, p. 265.

13. *Ibid.*, pp. 277, 303.

14. *Ibid.*, p. 281.

15. Cf. Manly's statement in *The Plain-Dealer*: "as a Coward is more bloody than a brave Man, a fool is more malicious than a Man of Wit." *Ibid.*, p. 499.

16. *Ibid.*, pp. 304, 335.

17. *Ibid.* See Pinchwife's speeches, pp. 293, 310; Sparkish's, p. 304; Lady Fidget's, p. 350. Horner continues her comparison, which is appropriate to the kind of "love" they are talking about.

18. *Ibid.*, p. 304.

19. Even Pinchwife's leading his wife to Horner, although indeed a gross improbability, may be partly justified on the same grounds: Pinchwife is so absorbed in calculations about disposing of his women with least trouble to himself that he does not notice what is going on before his eyes.

20. *Ibid.*, pp. 334, 345, 346.

21. *Ibid.*, pp. 268, 293.

22. *Ibid.*, p. 280.

23. *Ibid.*, pp. 269, 282, 318-19. Milton, *Paradise Lost*, IV, 637-38.

24. Wycherley, *Plays*, pp. 323, 341.

25. *Ibid.*, pp. 271, 332.

26. *Ibid.*, pp. 270, 301.

27. *Ibid.*, pp. 308, 338.

28. *Ibid.*, p. 286.

29. P. F. Vernon, *William Wycherley* (London, 1965), pp. 26, 28.

30. Wycherley, *Plays*, pp. 274, 309.

31. *Ibid.*, p. 313.

32. Sermon XLII (c. 1690), quoted by D. Judson Milburn, *The Age of Wit: 1650-1750* (New York, 1966), p. 291.

33. Etherege, *Dramatic Works*, p. 201.

34. Rochester, *Poems*, pp. 82-83.

35. Wycherley, *Plays*, pp. 347-48.

36. *Ibid.*, pp. 332, 334.

37. *Ibid.*, pp. 276, 358.

38. *Ibid.*, p. 263.

39. The specific plot borrowings are: (1) Sganarelle carries a letter from Isabella to Valère, believing it is a letter from Valère which Isabella is returning unopened; he incongruously gloats over Valère, as Pinchwife does over Horner when he brings him a love letter from

Margery, thinking it is an insulting letter. (2) Sganarelle leads Isabella to Valère, thinking she is her sister Léonor, as Pinchwife leads Margery to Horner, thinking she is her sister-in-law Alithea. Also, Isabella and Valère court before the face of the unwitting Sganarelle, as Harcourt woos Alithea in front of Sparkish.

40. It seems to me extremely unlikely that *The Plain-Dealer* was written before *The Country-Wife*, as Pope said. The obvious development of Wycherley's work is toward more and more definite moral purpose: from tentative beginnings in the early plays, to the balance between comedy and morality in *The Country-Wife*, to the intense moral seriousness and disgust with the age in *The Plain-Dealer*. I cannot believe that Wycherley regained the balance of *The Country-Wife* after writing *The Plain-Dealer*, while it is understandable that he had no place to go after *The Plain-Dealer*. Against Pope's word, which is generally unreliable about the chronology of Wycherley's plays, there is also the fact that *The Country-Wife* was produced two years before *The Plain-Dealer*, and there is the defense of *The Country-Wife* in *The Plain-Dealer*. It is conceivable that Wycherley withheld *The Plain-Dealer* from production for several years and that he inserted the defense of *The Country-Wife* years after writing the rest of the play; but surely this theory entails unnecessary complications. Wycherley would have had to insert two other afterthoughts had he written *The Plain-Dealer* before *The Country-Wife*: Novel's reference to Shadwell's *The Libertine* (produced in 1675) and Oldfox's to the government's order for closing the coffeehouses in November, 1675.

Chapter Four

1. Although modern commentators tend to see Alceste as a completely sympathetic hero, I believe that this is a romantic misreading. It seems to me that Alceste is a consistently comic figure, despite his admirable and sympathetic aspects, and I find no evidence that his foil, Philinte, is less than ideal. The most definite signs that Manly is presented primarily as a sympathetic hero—the criticism of Freeman and the wish-fulfillment ending—contrast sharply with the presentation of Philinte and the ending of *Le Misanthrope*. For further comment on Wycherley's modifications of *Le Misanthrope*, see Norman Suckling, "Molière and English Restoration Comedy," *Stratford-upon-Avon Studies 6* (London, 1965), pp. 94-95, and A. M. Friedson, "Wycherley and Molière: Satirical Point of View in *The Plain-Dealer*," *Modern Philology*, LXIV (1967), 189-97.

Wycherley got the idea for his defense of *The Country-Wife* in Act II from Molière's *Critique of The School for Wives*, and for the scene in which Oldfox and the Widow Blackacre torment each other with their respective writings (Act IV) from Scarron's *City-Romance* or perhaps its original, Furetière's *Le Roman bourgeois*. Just as Wycherley dedicated *The Plain-Dealer* to a bawd, Furetière dedicated his work to the public executioner, ironically praising him as an eminent citizen. See M. J. O'Regan, "Furetière and Wycherley," *Modern Language Review*, LIII (1958), 77-81. Wycherley's dedication is also indebted to Montaigne's essay "Upon Some Verses of Virgil" (III, 5), as Howard Mumford Jones pointed out in "Wycherley, Montaigne, Tertullian, and Mr. Summers," *Modern Language Notes*, XLVII (1932), 244-45. Fidelia derives ultimately from Viola in Shakespeare's *Twelfth Night*, but she has many prototypes. The Widow Blackacre may have been inspired by Racine's Comtesse de Pimbesche in *The Litigants*, but in all significant respects she is an original creation.

2. Wycherley, *Plays*, p. 397.

3. Although Shadwell claimed that his play was indebted only to Molière's *The Bores*, he obviously derived the Stanford-Lovel relationship from *Le Misanthrope*. His play, however, lacks the serious moral import of either *Le Misanthrope* or *The Plain-Dealer*. Shadwell's Poet Ninny resembles Novel, Woodcock is very like Lord Plausible, and Emilia is what Olivia pretends to be. Wycherley may have got from this play a plot idea for *The Gentleman Dancing-Master*: Sir Positive, finding himself married to Lovel's former whore, pretends he married her knowingly, just as Wycherley's positive Don Diego pretends he knew all along about his daughter's clandestine courtship, so no one can challenge his penetration.

4. Wycherley, *Plays*, p. 389.

5. *Ibid.*, pp. 394, 395. However, extreme as Manly's statement is, it is very close to one of Wycherley's own maxims: "There is no great, or true Friendship, but what is particular, and has but one Object of its Love" (Wycherley, *Works*, IV, 116, and cf. IV, 37).

6. *Plays*, pp. 462, 470.

7. *Ibid.*, p. 424.

8. *Ibid.*, p. 496.

9. *Ibid.*, pp. 386, 515. Norman N. Holland maintains that Wycherley intentionally represented two levels of meaning in *The Plain-Dealer*: while the play as a whole is realistic, its ending hints at an ideal world. He compares Manly's ultimate triumph to that of the protagonist of a Chaplin film, forgetting that Wycherley's comedy, unlike Chaplin's, explicitly claimed to be realistic. See *First Modern Comedies*, pp. 101, 108-9.

Notes and References

10. Chorney traces the character of Manly to a type described by seventeenth-century character writers, in "Wycherley's Manly Reinterpreted," *Essays Critical and Historical Dedicated to Lily B. Campbell* (Berkeley, 1950), pp. 161-69; Lott, to the humors characters of Jonson, in "A Comparative Study of the Humors Character in the Comedies of Ben Jonson and William Wycherley" (Nashville, Tenn., 1962); and Rose Zimbardo, to the bitter malcontent of Jacobean satiric drama, who was at once the object and spokesman of satire, in *Wycherley's Drama*, pp. 77-89. Holland analyzes Manly in *The First Modern Comedies*, pp. 98-99, 105-6; Dobrée, in *Restoration Comedy* (London, 1924), pp. 80-81, 87-89; Wilson, in *A Preface to Restoration Drama* (Boston, 1965), pp. 160-63.

11. Wycherley, *Plays*, pp. 387, 431, 453.

12. *Ibid.*, pp. 410, 413-14, 417-18. John Dennis first pointed out how Wycherley made Novel appear to be contributing wit without being really witty; see *Critical Works*, II, 233-34. The occasion for Dennis's analysis was his indignant defense of Wycherley against a charge which he believed Dryden was making in an essay of 1695: "I know a poet, whom out of respect I will not name, who, being too witty himself, could draw nothing but wits in a comedy of his; even his fools were infected with the disease of their author. They overflowed with smart reparties, and were only distinguished from the intended wits by being called coxcombs." See Dryden, *Essays*, II, 142. Although this criticism seems less applicable to Wycherley than to Etherege or Congreve, most contemporaries—Pope and Abel Boyer, as well as Dennis—thought Dryden was alluding to Wycherley. See Alexander Pope, *Pastoral Poetry and An Essay on Criticism*, ed. E. Audra and Aubrey Williams (London, 1961), p. 80n; and *Letters of Wit, Politicks and Morality*, ed. Abel Boyer (London, 1701), p. 217.

13. Wycherley, *Plays*, pp. 414, 427, 482. The second remark was inspired by a speech by Célimène in *Le Misanthrope*, II: *Eight Plays by Molière*, trans. Morris Bishop (New York, 1957), p. 246.

14. Wycherley, *Plays*, p. 493.

15. *Ibid.*, p. 467. Wycherley's Olivia seems to be a hideous travesty of Shakespeare's Olivia in *Twelfth Night* (whence he borrowed Fidelia), who likewise embarrassed a girl disguised as a boy by falling in love with her. Although the two Olivias seem entirely different, there was probably some (unconscious?) connection in Wycherley's mind between them. Perhaps it was his revulsion at the woman who takes an aggressive role in sexual affairs.

16. *Ibid.*, pp. 406, 465; Dryden, *Three Plays*, pp. 326-27.

17. Wycherley, *Plays,* pp. 139, 408.

18. *Ibid.,* p. 386.

19. Rose Zimbardo justifies Fidelia as an essential part of the satiric structure, representing the ideal—faith, love—which contrasts with the revolting behavior found everywhere else in the play (*Wycherley's Drama,* pp. 144-45). But if Fidelia is accepted as a symbol, her relationship with Manly must be justified in symbolic terms. How, if Manly is not only a satyr but one who succumbs to the very hypocrisy he declaims against, can he be ultimately united with ideal faith?

20. Anne Righter argues that the nihilism of *The Plain-Dealer,* an accentuation of the nihilism she finds in *The Country-Wife,* resulted not from Wycherley's personal psychological conflicts but from "a change in the temper of the age," toward "bitter railing . . . passion, and . . . abandonment to excess." But the superbly balanced *Man of Mode* was produced in the same year as *The Plain-Dealer,* and Congreve's equally balanced and successful comedies many years later. It seems to me that the distinction she draws results from differences in quality rather than progress over time: Wycherley was temperamentally unsuited to write comedies as urbane as Etherege's and Congreve's, and no other dramatist of the period had the necessary very high literary ability. See "William Wycherley," *Restoration Dramatists,* pp. 118-22.

21. Rose Zimbardo believes that *The Plain-Dealer* is a satire on hypocrisy; Willard Connely, on false friendship. See *Wycherley's Drama,* p. 86 and Willard Connely, *Brawny Wycherley* (New York, 1930), pp. 116-19. P. F. Vernon believes that *The Plain-Dealer* fails not because of its ambitious aim, but because Wycherley lacked sufficient knowledge of society to indict it as a whole and was unable to find an adequate positive contrast to social corruption. See *William Wycherley,* pp. 34-35.

22. Wycherley, *Plays,* pp. 410, 462-63.

23. Pepys, *Diary,* II, 88.

24. Wycherley, *Plays,* p. 396.

25. *Ibid.,* pp. 439, 444, 445.

26. *Ibid.,* pp. 448-49.

27. *Ibid.,* pp. 438, 473.

28. *Ibid.,* pp. 473, 474, 513-14.

29. *London Stage 1660–1800: Part I,* p. 253, says this was probably the premiere.

30. Thomas Davies's comment reinforces my position: "From Mohun's generally acting grave, solemn, and austere parts, I should

have cast him into that of Manly in the Plain Dealer; but it seems Hart claimed it. . . . In . . . The Country Wife, Pinchwife, a part not unallied in humour to Manly, was acted by Mohun." See *Dramatic Miscellanies*, III, 262. The general attitude toward Manly seems to have changed by Davies's time; see Chapter 7, note 4.

31. Wycherley, *Plays*, p. 380.
32. Dennis, *Critical Works*, II, 277. According to Matthew Prior, Wycherley owed it to Dorset "that the Town liked his *Plain Dealer*"; see the dedication to his *Poems on Several Occasions* (London, 1718).
33. Dryden, *Essays*, I, 182.
34. E.g., Dennis (*Critical Works*, I, 40-41, 224), Boyer (*Letters*, p. 217), and Charles Gildon, in *The Lives and Characters of the English Dramatic Poets . . . begun by Mr. Langbain . . . and continued* (by Gildon) (London, 1699), p. 150. Among modern critics W. C. Ward and Rose Zimbardo believe *The Plain-Dealer* to be Wycherley's masterpiece.
35. Wycherley, *Plays*, p. 493.
36. *The Rochester-Savile Letters*, ed. John Harold Wilson (Columbus, Ohio, 1941), p. 33. In a poem called "Plain Dealings Downfall" (c. 1680), Rochester represented Plain-dealing as a destitute girl driven from door to door (everyone knowing that "he that entertain'd her must be poor"), until finally she dies, "whil's Knavery Laughing, Rung her passing Bell." See Rochester, *Poems*, p. 125.
37. Halifax, *Complete Works*, p. 228.
38. Wycherley, *Plays*, p. 386.
39. Halifax, *Works*, 14; *Savile Correspondence: Letters to and from Henry Savile*, ed. William D. Cooper (London, 1858), p. 150.
40. *Critical Essays of the Seventeenth Century*, ed. J. E. Spingarn (Oxford, 1908), III, 244.
41. Dryden, *Essays*, II, 84.
42. William Congreve, *Complete Plays*, ed. Alexander Ewald (New York, 1956), pp. 196-97.
43. Rose Zimbardo, who points out this resemblance, believes that Malevole and similar characters were primarily objects of satire. Although Altofront is obviously a sympathetic hero, Malevole, his false, assumed personality, is both comic and subjected to severe criticism. See *Wycherley's Drama*, pp. 73-77. I do not see such a sharp distinction between Altofront and Malevole, who seems, rather, to represent the side of Altofront brought out by treason and adversity. Moreover, Malevole is criticized only by the vicious characters in the play. Further evidence of the seventeenth-century sympathy for sullen antisocial types is Congreve's remark that Ben Jonson's obvi-

ously comic Morose is ridiculous only because of the excess of his humour: "If the Poet had given him but a Moderate proportion . . . 'tis odds but half the Audience would have sided with the Character and have Condemn'd the Author for Exposing a Humour that was neither Remarkable nor Ridiculous" (*Critical Essays of the Seventeenth Century*, III, 247).

44. Pope, *Poems*, p. 220.

45. Thomas Shadwell, Dedication to *The Virtuoso*, *The Complete Works*, ed. Montague Summers (London, 1927), III, 101. Restoration critics used the term "humour" confusingly, sometimes inconsistently. I have tried to explain the essential meaning of the term, as they used it; but there are no firm lines of distinction. Dorimant and Millamant, who are certainly as well drawn as any characters in Wycherley, would seem by my definition to be manners characters, since they are the quintessence of the Restoration beau and belle. In the Prologue to *Bury Fair* Shadwell, who in general condemned the characterization in the contemporary comedy of manners, made a point of praising Etherege's Sir Frederick Frolic, Lady Cockwood, and Sir Fopling Flutter as excellent "humours." (He also listed Manly, a "humours" character by any definition.)

46. Dryden, *Essays*, I, 139. Dryden had no doubt that Jonson was the greatest of English comic playwrights (*ibid.*, 137-38).

47. Vernon, *William Wycherley*, p. 13.

Chapter Five

1. Dryden, "To My Dear Friend, Mr. Congreve, On his Comedy Called the Double Dealer," *Poems*, p. 167. Cf. "To Mr. Southern," where he advised Southerne to imitate the style of Etherege and the wit of Wycherley (*ibid.*, p. 166).

2. E.g., in letters to Pope and Dennis. See Alexander Pope, *The Correspondence*, ed. George Sherburn (Oxford, 1956), I, 55, 66, 69, 80 and Wycherley, *Complete Works*, II, 199.

3. *Miscellany Poems . . . By the Most Eminent Hands, Published by Mr. Dryden* (London, 1716), II, 101.

4. Richardson Pack, "Some Memoirs of William Wycherley Esq.," introduction to *The Posthumous Works of William Wycherley*, ed. Lewis Theobald (London, 1728), p. 9.

5. Lansdowne (Gildon, really), *Memoirs . . . of Wycherley*, pp. 20, 22. Cf. Lansdowne's *Genuine Works*, II, 110, 113, and Dennis, *Letters*, pp. 8, 10-11.

6. Dennis, *Letters*, p. 40.

7. *Ibid.*, p. 18.
8. Pack, "Memoirs," *Posthumous Works*, p. 9.
9. Wycherley, *Works*, IV, 26.
10. Dennis, *Critical Works*, II, 411.
11. Etherege, *Letterbook*, p. 356. Dryden's reference to "apoplexy" was presumably a careless misremembering of what had happened to Wycherley. Although the symptoms of apoplexy and encephalitis are completely different, they are alike in that both are acute conditions which often leave permanent mental damage. Dryden was not at this time intimate with Wycherley (who had been in the Fleet Prison for four years), so could easily have forgotten precisely what had ailed him.
12. Spence, *Anecdotes*, p. 2.
13. *Ibid.*, p. 121.
14. Dennis, *Critical Works*, II, 411.
15. John Locke, "Thoughts on Education," quoted in *Social England*, ed. H. D. Traill and J. S. Mann (New York, 1909), IV, Sect. 2, 680.
16. Hamilton, *Memoirs of . . . Gramont*, pp. 270-71.
17. Dennis, *Critical Works*, II, 411.
18. W. G. Hargest, "Wycherley and the Countess of Drogheda," *Times Literary Supplement* (November 21, 1929), p. 960.
19. Connely, *Brawny Wycherley*, pp. 161, 163.
20. Hargest, "Wycherley and the Countess of Drogheda," *Times Literary Supplement* (November 21, 1929), p. 960, with corrections by Eleanore Boswell, *ibid.* (November 28, 1929), pp. 1001-1002.
21. Dennis, *Critical Works*, II, 411. Cf. Pepys's diary entry for June 6, 1665, indicating that Lady Sandwich was waiting for notice from the king whether her son might court the heiress Miss Malet (later Lady Rochester).
22. Hargest, "Wycherley and the Countess of Drogheda," *Times Literary Supplement* (November 21, 1929), with corrections by Boswell, *ibid.* (November 28, 1929), pp. 1001-1002.
23. Wycherley, *Works*, III, 195-97.
24. Dennis, *Critical Works*, II, 412.
25. Wycherley, *Works*, III, 153, IV, 192. Wycherley also wrote an unusually large number of poems on impotence; see *Works*, III, 36-37, 182-83, 201-2, 259-60; IV, 249-50.
26. *Ibid.*, III, 87.
27. Connely, *Brawny Wycherley*, pp. 180-81. The situation was complicated by the fact that Laetitia-Isabella's nephew, who had succeeded as earl of Radnor in February, 1682, had married the daughter

of a rich miser, Sir John Cutler (immortalized by Pope in his third Moral Essay), who refused to give her a dowry. This may have increased his reluctance to let any of his aunt's estate go to Wycherley. Wycherley wrote a poem to Cutler, an ironical encomium on avarice (*Works*, IV, 234-36).

28. Lansdowne (really Gildon), *Memoirs of . . . Wycherley*, p. 13.

29. Wycherley, *Works*, II, 261. The *Epistles* were published in 1683.

30. *Ibid.*, II, 249, 250.

31. *Ibid.*, II, 249, 258, 259.

32. *Ibid.*, II, 270.

33. Wycherley followed up his epistle "To the King" with "To the King my Master; after His Mercy, to a Fault, shown to some Conspirators against his Power and Life," presumably written after the revelation of the Rye House Plot (1683). The poem was as adulatory as would be expected, but probably the king never saw it, as it must have been written in prison and was not published until the *Miscellany Poems* of 1704.

34. Dennis, *Critical Works*, II, 230.

35. Wycherley, *Works*, IV, 41-45.

36. The only extant order for Wycherley's commitment is dated July, 1685; but this must have been a recommitment. Records were not kept before 1685. All authorities agree that Wycherley was imprisoned shortly after his wife's death, and he would hardly have remained in Newgate.

37. It is even said that George was committed at his own father's suit. See Garbet, *History of Wem*, p. 156.

38. Pack, "Memoirs," *Posthumous Works*, p. 10.

39. *The Oeconomy of the Fleet*, ed. Augustus Jessopp (London, 1879), p. 99.

40. Strype wrote in 1720: "This Prison . . . is only dreadful to such poor Men as have parted with their All to their Creditors, and left themselves Nothing to subsist on." See John Stow, *A Survey of the Cities of London and Westminster*, corrected by John *Strype* (London, 1754). I, 754.

41. Wycherley, *Works*, III, 272-75.

42. Allen, "Two Wycherley Letters," *Times Literary Supplement* (April 18, 1935), p. 257.

43. Spence, *Anecdotes*, p. 34.

44. Lansdowne (really Gildon), *Memoirs of . . . Wycherley*, p. 8; Pack, "Memoirs," *Posthumous Works*, p. 11.

45. Lansdowne (really Gildon), *Memoirs of . . . Wycherley*, p. 8.

46. John Dryden, *The Letters,* ed. Charles E. Ward (Durham, N.C., 1942), pp. 73-74.
47. Dennis, *Letters,* pp. 28-29.
48. Pope, *Correspondence,* I, 73.
49. Spence, *Anecdotes,* p. 10.
50. Letter of December 27, 1688 to Colonel James Grahme, quoted in Connely's *Brawny Wycherley,* pp. 211-14.
51. Congreve, *Plays,* p. 37.
52. Dryden, *Essays,* II, 77; *Miscellany Poems* (1716), IV, 64. Cf. Pope, *Correspondence,* III, 363.
53. Howard P. Vincent, "The Death of William Wycherley," *Harvard Studies and Notes in Philology and Literature,* XV (1933), 222.
54. Lansdowne (really Gildon), *Memoirs of . . . Wycherley,* p. 21.
55. Vincent, "Death of Wycherley," *Harvard Studies,* XV (1933), pp. 224-25. According to Shrimpton, Barnes was suing for wages in arrear which Wycherley had actually paid him, but mislaid the receipts. See William Egerton, *Faithful Memoirs of the Life . . . of Mrs. Anne Oldfield* (London, 1731), pp. 122-23. Perhaps much of Wycherley's apparent extravagance and irresponsibility in his later years resulted from people's taking advantage of him because he could no longer keep his accounts straight.
56. *London Stage 1660-1800, Part I* and *Part II, passim.* Some of these dates are for new editions of the plays, but the editors believe these indicate performances. Since the records are incomplete, particularly for the seventeenth century, the plays were probably performed more often.
57. *Critical Essays of the Seventeenth Century,* III, 196.
58. Jeremy Collier, *A Short View of the Immorality, and Profaneness of the English Stage* (London, 1698), pp. 173-74.
59. Richard Steele, *The Tatler,* #3 (April 16, 1709), #9 (April 30, 1709). In *Spectator* #266 Steele praised the dedication to *The Plain-Dealer* as "a Master-piece of Raillery" on bawds.
60. *Letters of Wit, Politicks and Morality,* ed. Boyer, p. 217.
61. Quoted by Henry B. Wheatley, *London Past and Present* (London, 1891), I, 316.
62. Harris, *Charles Sackville, Sixth Earl of Dorset,* p. 196. Others included were Dryden, Congreve, Betterton, Mohun, and Dorset himself.
63. Spence tells a tale that Kneller first drew Wycherley "with his little straggling grey hair: he could not bear it when done, and Sir Godfrey was obliged to draw a wig to it" (*Anecdotes,* p. 255). How-

ever, the portrait definitely shows Wycherley in his own hair. The portrait, which is now at Knole Park, is reproduced in Michael Morris, Lord Killanin's *Sir Godfrey Kneller and his Times* (London, 1948).

64. Dryden, *Essays*, II, 144.

65. Wycherley, *Works*, IV, 155-60.

66. Quoted by George Sherburn, *The Early Career of Alexander Pope* (Oxford, 1934), p. 54. (Pope also greatly valued Walsh's literary judgment.) Dryden, *Essays*, II, 138; "Walsh, William" and "Moyle, Walter," *Dictionary of National Biography*.

67. Pope, *Poems*, p. 257. (Granville was created Baron Lansdowne in 1711). *Miscellany Poems* (1716), IV, 24. Both Congreve and Moyle referred in letters to their friendship with Wycherley; see William Congreve, *Letters and Documents*, ed. John C. Hodges (New York, 1964), pp. 91, 192.

68. Dennis, *Critical Works*, II, 411; Dennis, *Letters*, 7.

69. Dennis, *Letters*, pp. 31-33.

70. *Ibid.*, p. 34. After Dryden's death, Wycherley's friendship with Dennis must have cooled. Dennis would not have publicly referred to Wycherley as an "ancient Wit" possessed by an evil specter (Pope), as he did in his *Reflections . . . upon . . . An Essay upon Criticism* (1711), if they had still been close friends. See *Critical Works*, I, 416.

Chapter Six

1. He said in his Postscript to *Miscellany Poems* that he wrote the book "when 'twas not so much my Head's Need to Write, as my Pocket's." See Wycherley, *Works*, III, 14.

2. *The Plain-Dealer, Plays*, p. 406; Harley Granville-Barker, *On Dramatic Method* (New York, 1956), p. 126.

3. John Dryden, *The Letters*, ed. Charles E. Ward (Durham, N.C., 1942), p. 54.

4. Cf. Granville's less judicious evaluation: Wycherley was "no Master of Numbers" and seemed "to despise all Ornament but intrinsick Merit," but his truth to nature made up for this deficiency. See Lansdowne, *Genuine Works*, II, 111-12.

5. Howard P. Vincent, "William Wycherley's *Miscellany Poems*," *Philological Quarterly*, XVI (1937), 145-48. A letter from Wycherley to Charles Montagu, earl of Halifax (May 12, 1704), indicates the embarrassing complications associated with the issuing of *Miscellany Poems*. Halifax had subscribed to the book when it was first advertised, but Briscoe never informed Wycherley of the fact. After *Miscellany Poems* finally appeared, Dr. Garth told Wycherley that Hali-

fax had subscribed, and so Wycherley sent him a copy. The letter suggests that Wycherley was personally acquainted with Halifax. See Wycherley, *Works*, II, 242.

6. Wycherley, *Works*, III, 3, 17, 279.

7. Alexander Pope, *The Correspondence*, ed. George Sherburn (Oxford, 1956), I, 16.

8. "The Apology; To his Ingenious Friend" and "An Epistle to a Witty Friend. . . . " "An Epistle from the Country, to my Friend Sir C. S." and "An Epistle from the Country, in Answer to one from the Town" are too close in idea and phrasing to the first pair. Wycherley, *Works*, III, 121-22, 128-29, 189, 208-9.

9. Wycherley, *Works*, III, 132-33, 156, 231.

10. John Dryden, *Poems*, p. 171; *Essays*, ed. W. P. Ker (New York, 1961), II, 84.

11. Wycherley, *Plays*, 270-71, 431, 452. Of course the similes of fops like Sparkish are supposed to be labored—but not those of the true wits.

12. Pope, *Correspondence*, I, 16. Wycherley, *Works*, IV, 226.

13. Wycherley, *Works*, III, 103-9. Pope mentioned this as one of Wycherley's better poems, along with "In Praise of Laziness" and "In Praise of Ignorance" (*Correspondence*, I, 15). This poem had been separately issued early in 1704 as *The Folly of Industry, or, The Busy Man Expos'd*. Supposed to have been "Dropt in the Publick Walks of the New Exchange," it was perhaps a trial balloon. It was reissued in 1705, after the publication of *Miscellany Poems*, under the title it had in that volume (Summers's note in Wycherley, *Works*, III, 279).

14. Lansdowne, *Works*, II, 113. In the same letter he refers to Wycherley's "*Horatian* Wit." Pope wrote to Henry Cromwell in 1709: my dog "follows me about as constantly here in the Country, as I was us'd to do Mr. Wycherley in the Towne" (*Correspondence*, I, 73).

15. Quoted by Wheatley, *London Past and Present*, III, 520.

16. He proudly cited this example of loyalty in "A Letter to the Publisher" of *The Dunciad*, which James Sutherland attributes to Pope himself; see Alexander Pope, *The Dunciad*, ed. James Sutherland (London, 1963), pp. xxv, 19.

17. Alexander Pope, *Minor Poems*, ed. Norman Ault and John Butt (London, 1954), pp. 37-38. Wycherley himself retaliated against Ozell and Rowe in his poem "The Bill of Fare," which was not published during his lifetime; see *Works*, IV, 226.

18. Pope, *Correspondence*, I, 3, 12, 14.

19. *Ibid.*, I, 13.

20. *Ibid.*, I, 83, 29.

21. *Ibid.*, I, 31-32, 33. Pope was very unhappy about the publication of Wycherley's *Posthumous Works* in 1728, feeling they reflected on both himself and Wycherley, since neither had believed them worthy of publication (*ibid.*, III, 54-55). Pope's work on Wycherley's poem on dullness may have provided the initial inspiration for *The Dunciad;* for Wycherley's poem, see *Works,* IV, 69, 152-53.

22. Pope, *Correspondence,* I, 34.

23. *Ibid.*, I, 58.

24. *Ibid.*, I, 73, 77, 78-82, 83, 84-85.

25. Wycherley, *Plays,* p. 385. Pope, *Poems,* p. 258.

26. Wycherley, *Works,* II, 275; Pope, *Correspondence,* I, 83; Pope, *Poems,* pp. 66-67. E. Audra and Aubrey Williams point out further echoes in their edition of Pope's *Pastoral Poetry and An Essay on Criticism* (London, 1961), pp. 268, 275, 279, 281.

27. Pope, *Correspondence,* I, 134. This would suggest that lines 604-9 of the *Essay,* which compare a superannuated poet who persists in rhyming to a person straining to defecate, do not allude to Wycherley, although Dennis charged that they did. It is hard to believe Pope guilty of such treachery, especially as he was all along professing friendship for Wycherley. Unconsciously, however, his frustration over fussing with Wycherley's senile efforts might have contributed to the venom of the lines.

28. *Ibid.*, I, 256.

29. *Ibid.*, I, 102, 55.

30. Wycherley, *Works,* IV, 108.

31. *Ibid.*, IV, 121, 134, 136, 138-39; La Rochefoucauld, *Maxims,* trans. Louis Kronenberger (New York, 1959), p. 48.

32. Wycherley, *Works,* IV, 72, 150-51.

33. Spence, *Anecdotes,* p. 13.

34. Vincent, "The Death of William Wycherley," *Harvard Studies,* p. 223.

35. Pope, *Correspondence,* I, 70.

36. *Ibid.*, I, 329. On one of Pope's two last visits to him, Wycherley made a quip which Pope thought worthy of repeating to Swift ten years later: one has to expect mischief from great oppressors, "But to be Squirted to death . . . by *Potecaries Prentices,* by the under Strappers of Under Secretaries, to Secretaries, who were no Secretaries—this would provoke as dull a dog as Ph[ilip]s himself" (*Correspondence,* II, 350). Pack and Gildon also believed that Wycherley married voluntarily; see Pack, "Memoirs of William Wycherley Esq.," introduction to *Posthumous Works,* p. 13, and Lansdowne (really Gildon), *Memoirs of . . . Wycherley,* pp. 21-22.

37. Vincent, "Death of William Wycherley," *Harvard Studies,* pp. 224-36, 240-41. Shrimpton justified his relationship with Wycherley in every respect in a public letter printed in Egerton's *Memoirs . . . of Mrs. Anne Oldfield,* pp. 122-25, representing himself, not very convincingly, as Wycherley's selfless and only friend during his last months.

Chapter Seven

1. Emmett L. Avery, *"The Country-Wife* in the Eighteenth Century," *Research Studies of the State College of Washington,* X (March, 1942), 147, 152, 156-57, 167. In the summer of 1718, *Love in a Wood* was acted twice at Drury Lane, apparently its last productions.

2. John McClain, *Journal American* (November 29, 1957); Brooks Atkinson, *New York Times* (November 28, 1957); Walter Kerr, *Herald Tribune* (November 28, 1957).

3. Richard Watts, *New York Post* (December 10, 1965); Howard Taubman, *New York Times* (December 10, 1965).

4. Benjamin Victor, *Memoirs of the Life of Barton Booth* (1733), quoted by Emmett L. Avery, *"The Plain-Dealer* in the Eighteenth Century," *Research Studies of the State College of Washington,* XI (1943), 240. In the mid-eighteenth century, James Quin shone in the parts of Pinchwife and Manly. See Emmett L. Avery, "The Reputation of Wycherley's Comedies as Stage Plays in the Eighteenth Century," *Research Studies of the State College of Washington,* XII (1944), 141.

5. Voltaire, *Philosophical Letters,* trans. Ernest Dilworth (Indianapolis, 1961), pp. 91, 93 (Letter XIX). Voltaire believed that *The Plain-Dealer* was fully equal to *Le Misanthrope* of his countryman Molière: he said that Wycherley's play gained in force what it lost in elegance and that "The English author corrected the only fault in Molière's play, its lack of plot and interest."

6. Avery, *"Plain-Dealer," Research Studies,* XI (1943), 244, 245, Appendix; Avery, *"Country-Wife," Research Studies,* X (1942), 142.

7. Lansdowne (really Gildon), *Memoirs of . . . Wycherley,* p. 4.

8. Letter to Pope of 1709, in Pope, *Correspondence,* I, 61.

9. Wycherley, *Works,* IV, 17-18.

10. *Ibid.,* III, 10.

11. Dennis, *Critical Works,* II, 121.

12. Wycherley, *Plays,* p. 406.

13. See, for example, his presentation of the three young men in *Epsom Wells* and of the heroes of *The Squire of Alsatia* and *The Scowrers.*

Selected Bibliography

PRIMARY SOURCES

1. Editions of Complete Works

SUMMERS, MONTAGUE, ed. *The Complete Works of William Wycherley.* New York: Russell and Russell, 1964. 4 vols. This edition, originally published in 1924, is textually unreliable and capriciously annotated, but is at present the only one.

Professor ARTHUR FRIEDMAN of the University of Chicago is currently preparing an edition of Wycherley's complete works.

2. Editions of Selected Works

WARD, WILLIAM, ed. *William Wycherley.* London: Vizetelly, 1888. The Mermaid edition of Wycherley's plays.

WEALES, GERALD, ed. *The Complete Plays of William Wycherley.* Garden City, New York: Anchor Books, Doubleday, 1966. The New York University Press has published the same edition in hard covers. This is the best edition of the plays, with excellent notes.

Of the several separate editions of *The Country-Wife* and *The Plain-Dealer,* the best are G. B. Churchill's of the two plays (Boston: Heath, 1924) and the Regents Restoration Drama Series editions of *The Country-Wife,* ed. Thomas H. Fujimura (Lincoln: University of Nebraska Press, 1965), and *The Plain-Dealer,* ed. Leo Hughes (Lincoln: University of Nebraska Press, 1967).

SECONDARY SOURCES

1. Biographies

CONNELY, WILLARD. *Brawny Wycherley.* New York: Scribners, 1930. Popular biography, revealing superficial knowledge of the period and of Wycherley's works; at present, the only full-length biography.

PERROMAT, CHARLES. *William Wycherley: Sa Vie—son Oeuvre.* Paris: F. Alcan, 1921. More scholarly, but now outdated; in French.

The two most important specialized biographical studies are:

ALLEN, ROBERT J. "Two Wycherley Letters," *Times Literary Supplement,* April 18, 1935, p. 257. First printing of two important letters to Mulgrave.

VINCENT, HOWARD P. "The Death of William Wycherley," *Harvard Studies and Notes in Philology and Literature,* XV (1933), 219-42. Provides previously unknown details about Wycherley's last months.

2. Critical Studies

CHORNEY, ALEXANDER H. "Wycherley's Manly Reinterpreted," *Essays Critical and Historical Dedicated to Lily B. Campbell.* Berkeley: University of California Press, 1950. The first to argue that Manly is a comic figure.

DOBREE, BONAMY. *Restoration Comedy: 1660-1720.* London: Oxford University Press, 1924. Excellent survey; presents Wycherley as a savage satirist, a "John Fox masquerading in the habiliments of a Charles Sedley."

FUJIMURA, THOMAS H. *The Restoration Comedy of Wit.* Princeton: Princeton University Press, 1952. Argues that Wycherley, like the other Restoration dramatists, consistently maintained a "naturalistic and witty point of view from first to last."

GRANVILLE-BARKER, HARLEY. "Wycherley and Dryden." *On Dramatic Method.* New York: Hill and Wang, 1956. Entertaining attack on *The Plain-Dealer.*

HAZLITT, WILLIAM. "On Wycherley, Congreve, Vanbrugh, and Farquhar." *Lectures on the English Comic Writers.* Garden City, New York: Doubleday, n.d. Remarkably enthusiastic, perceptive appreciation of Restoration comedy, considering its date (1819).

HOLLAND, NORMAN N. *The First Modern Comedies: The Significance of Etherege, Wycherley and Congreve.* Cambridge: Harvard University Press, 1959. Excellent close analysis; argues the plays are intellectually substantial and significant.

KNIGHTS, L. C. "Restoration Comedy: The Reality and the Myth." *Explorations.* London: Chatto and Windus, 1946. Withering attack on Restoration comedy as "trivial, gross and dull."

The London Stage 1660-1800. Part I: 1660-1700. Ed. William Van Lennep, with critical introduction by Emmett L. Avery and Arthur H. Scouten. *Part II: 1700-29.* Ed. with critical introduction by Emmett L. Avery. Carbondale: Southern Illinois

University Press, 1965, 1960. Provides voluminous details on Restoration theaters, performances of plays, and so on.

LYNCH, KATHLEEN. *The Social Mode of Restoration Drama.* New York: Macmillan, 1926. Good general discussion, particularly of the distinguishing characteristics of Restoration comedy.

MORRISSEY, L. J. "Wycherley's *Country Dance*," *Studies in English Literature,* VIII (1968), 415-29. Significance of the dance motif in *The Country-Wife.*

NICOLL, ALLARDYCE. *A History of Restoration Drama 1660-1700.* Cambridge: Cambridge University Press, 1928. Classic work on the theater of the period.

PALMER, JOHN. *The Comedy of Manners.* London: G. Bell, 1913. First analytic discussion of Restoration comedy.

RIGHTER, ANNE. "William Wycherley," *Stratford-upon-Avon Studies 6* (London, 1965). Argues that *The Country-Wife* and *The Plain-Dealer* are nihilistic, in tune with "a change in the temper of the age."

ROGERS, K. M. "Fatal Inconsistency: Wycherley and *The Plain-Dealer*," *English Literary History,* XXVIII (1961), 148-62. Argues that the play fails because of its inconsistencies.

VERNON, P. F. "Marriage of Convenience and The Moral Code of Restoration Comedy," *Essays in Criticism,* XII (1962), 370-87. Argues that Restoration comedy made a responsible attack on contemporary marriage customs.

———. *William Wycherley.* London: Longman's Green, 1965. Short but illuminating discussion.

WILCOX, JOHN. *The Relation of Molière to Restoration Comedy.* New York: Columbia University Press, 1938. Competent discussion of Molière's influence.

WILSON, JOHN H. *A Preface to Restoration Drama.* Boston: Houghton Mifflin, 1965. Excellent survey.

ZIMBARDO, ROSE. *Wycherley's Drama: A Link in the Development of English Satire.* New Haven: Yale University Press, 1965. Makes an ingenious and plausible case that Wycherley was writing dramatic satires in the tradition of Elizabethan "comicall satyre."

3. Studies of the Period

MACAULAY, THOMAS BABINGTON. *History of England from the Accession of James II.* London: J. M. Dent, 1906. 4 vols. Macaulay's opening chapter gives a highly unsympathetic but entertaining, learned, and generally sound picture of England in 1685.

A Restoration Reader. Ed. James Holly Hanford. New York: Grove
Press, 1960. Excellent collection of writings by varied people
of the Restoration.
WILSON, JOHN H. *The Court Wits of the Restoration.* Princeton:
Princeton University Press, 1948. Lively, authoritative survey
of its subject.

Index